A Little Book of
Prosperity Magic

By Cynthia Killion

This book belongs to:
Susan P. Rubin, DMD,HHC
A Better Way Holistic Health
(914) 864-1293

THE CROSSING PRESS
FREEDOM, CALIFORNIA

Copyright © 2001 Cynthia Killion
Cover illustration by Kimberly Parrish
Cover design by Nathan Walker
Printed in the U.S.A.

For information on bulk purchases or group discounts for this and other Crossing Press titles, please contact our Special Sales Manager at 800/777-1048. Visit our Web site: **www.crossingpress.com**

Library of Congress Cataloging-in-Publication Data

Killion, Cynthia.
    A little book of prosperity magic / by Cynthia Killion.
       p. cm.
    ISBN 1-58091-118-8 (pbk.)
    1. Wealth--Religious aspects. I. Title.

BL65.W42 K55 2001
133.4'43--dc21

                                        2001042120

                    0   9   8   7   6   5   4   3   2   1

Contents

Preface

Perhaps you've heard the saying, "You can't have it all," or maybe you've been told that you aren't smart enough, spiritual enough, attractive enough, or lucky enough to experience success. Haven't we all heard this at one time or another? But no matter where you started in life, you can experience perfect prosperity. No matter what your past or current situation, you have the ability to manifest all that your heart desires. For you are created in the divine image of God and Goddess, and you deserve to have prosperity.

My greatest hope is that this book will help you become aware of the perfect prosperity that already exists inside of you. Whether you are concerned about your career, your finances, your spirituality, or your relationships, the secret to infusing yourself with perfect prosperity is seeing yourself in a new light—seeing yourself as the powerful and truly divine child of the Universe that you really are! In reality, there is no need to create prosperity; there is only a need to manifest your inner prosperity.

Many Blessings!

Introduction

Prosperity. What do you think of when you hear that word? Many of us think of financial success or material goods. But prosperity is about much more than money. Love, knowledge, health, power, and a sense of personal meaning are all aspects of prosperity. In fact, true prosperity involves feeling fulfilled, not just wealthy. For most of us, it takes much more than money to be fulfilled. The purpose of this book is not only to help you increase your cash flow, but to help you expand your awareness of what prosperity really is.

Prosperity is a state of mind. Having prosperity means having an abundance consciousness and the ability to manifest all that you need at any given moment. Money or material things do not give you prosperity. Rather, it's the other way around: when your thoughts are aligned with the abundance of the Universe, you will naturally attract all that your heart desires. That's why manifesting prosperity always starts with changing your ideas.

If you want prosperity, then you must focus on opening yourself up as a channel for Universal Abundance. All prosperity comes from this Universal Abundance. Prosperity does not come from a job, investments, or profit-making schemes. The truth is that all these things are only vehicles or channels for Universal Energy; they are not the source of your prosperity. The source of your prosperity is within you. Therefore, you are always in control of how much prosperity you are manifesting for yourself. By choosing to be an open channel for Universal Energy, you can begin to create prosperity for yourself today.

When you are first beginning your prosperity work, go easy on yourself. Do not expect everything to change in the blink of an eye. Ease into your prosperity exercises slowly. Change is usually a series of many small steps followed by a few giant leaps. Even if you do not get the results you want at first, be gentle with yourself. It is your sustained effort over a period of time that will bring you true prosperity, not a few bursts of activity here and there. Remember: Manifesting prosperity is more like running a marathon than sprinting. It's staying in the race that's important, not how well your perform at the beginning.

CHAPTER 1

The Eight Principles of Prosperity

To start with, there are eight things about prosperity I would like to share with you. I believe these are the fundamental prosperity truths. If you familiarize yourself with these concepts, you will be well on your way to experiencing true prosperity.

1. You deserve prosperity. Furthermore, there is no reason you should have to work hard for it.
2. Struggle of any kind, financial or otherwise, is unnecessary.
3. True prosperity is always win–win. Others benefit when you are prosperous.
4. Poverty doesn't make you a better person. Generally, it only makes you a less happy person.
5. Prosperity is relative. What constitutes prosperity for me may not constitute prosperity for you.

6. Worrying about money does not create prosperity. It only creates a lack of money.

7. All prosperity is limitless and comes from the same source.

8. Prosperity comes from being open to Universal Abundance.

Just being exposed to these truths can help you release some of the common myths and fears surrounding prosperity. Let's explore each of these fundamental prosperity truths in more detail, and then you can jump right in with your first prosperity exercise.

YOU DESERVE PROSPERITY

Everyone does. However, you may have begun to doubt this. You may have even begun to believe that the reason that you don't already have prosperity is because you've done something wrong or have a moral defect. In truth, financial struggle or any other kind of struggle is rarely a reflection of moral defect. If you've had a hard time, it isn't necessarily because you are a bad person. (There are plenty of seemingly bad people who are financially prosperous.) Luckily, prosperity isn't something you have to earn through suffering or good deeds. It is something you claim by tuning your awareness into the abundance of the Universe.

You deserve to make a decent living and lead a joyous life. You deserve this not because of what you have done or haven't done, but because you are your own unique part of the Universe. You may have gotten the message from somewhere that you aren't good enough for prosperity or that prosperity isn't for you. However, I assure you that it is your divine right to have prosperity. Everyone deserves to have perfect prosperity, including you.

STRUGGLE IS UNNECESSARY

You do not have to struggle financially or any other way. Contrary to popular opinion, struggle, financial or otherwise, is not natural. Struggle often comes from unloving thought patterns, usually directed against the self. The Universe did not plan for us to struggle. True, some work and development of talent may be necessary for you to reap your highest prosperity, but the Universe did not decree that this work be burdensome or difficult. Usually, we experience struggle not because we have to, but because we begin to believe that we deserve to struggle or because we would rather struggle than receive things easily and effortlessly.

Metaphysicians have long known that we create our experiences with our beliefs. If you believe (for whatever reason) that you are destined to struggle, that you deserve to struggle, or that it is noble to struggle, then that is exactly what you will experience. On the other hand, if you change your thought patterns and tell yourself that you can experience life gently and effortlessly, then your experience of life will be gentle and effortless.

You may wonder why anybody, including you, could possibly believe that they deserve to struggle. One reason is that struggle has been glorified in our society. We have a lot of respect for people who experience great hardship on their way to success. We secretly and sometimes openly disdain those who seem to achieve their success without the proper amount of struggle, and call them names like "upstarts." The message we receive is that it is noble to struggle, and that if you don't have to fight or struggle for something, you are not worthy of having it.

What I would like to say to you is that there is nothing noble about struggle. Sure, it can make you feel angry, frustrated, and powerless. It also can make you feel heartbroken and downtrodden. If you have ever struggled, you know what I mean. To be fair, it can make you more determined, but it doesn't make you noble. Only fulfilling your soul purpose can do that.

Of course, achieving anything worthwhile, including prosperity, does require a certain amount of sustained effort, and the larger the goal, the more effort it will involve. But this is not the same as struggling. You do not have to beat your head against the wall at each and every turn. In fact, if you are doing something you love or trying to create something you love, it doesn't have to feel like effort at all. This is why when we say our prayers and affirmations, we can ask to receive something easily and effortlessly. The effort is still there, but by being open and clearing the channels for the Divine, we achieve what we want easily and without struggle. No matter who you are, it's not necessary to struggle.

TRUE PROSPERITY IS ALWAYS WIN–WIN

You do not have to worry that your prosperity will deprive other people of what they need. Nor do you have to worry that someone else must lose so that you can gain. The same power that created you has given you the ability to create true prosperity, while at the same time increasing the abundance available to everyone.

Every time you manifest something good for yourself, prosperity goes rippling out across the entire Universe. In other words, when you manifest true prosperity for yourself, the energy you send out helps increase the prosperity of everyone on the planet. I call this the trickle-around effect. This effect allows the benefits of your prosperity work to trickle around to those in need. That's why everyone wins when you are prosperous.

POVERTY DOESN'T MAKE YOU A BETTER PERSON

You do not have to experience scarcity or poverty. These things do not make you more spiritual or kind, nor do they necessarily make you a better person. Although you can choose to learn your lessons through poverty and suffering, the Universe would certainly prefer to give you prosperity and joy instead. Creation stands to gain nothing from your misery.

Our society is financially schizophrenic. We are told that it is good to try to get ahead in life and climb the ladder of success, but we are also told that it is noble to be poor. Unfortunately, poverty is a lot like struggling—those who have experienced it will tell you that there is nothing noble about it!

Denying yourself prosperity will serve only to make you into an economic martyr. It does absolutely nothing to help those less fortunate than you. In fact, when you resist the Universe's attempts to bring prosperity into your life, you become like a clogged drain, unable to pipe prosperity energy out either for yourself or for others. But when you open up to receive the blessings of the Universe, financial or otherwise, you become a giant prosperity pipeline, channeling out energy not only to yourself, but to others as well.

PROSPERITY IS RELATIVE

What prosperity means to me may not be the same thing it means to you. You have your own idea of what it means to experience true prosperity, even if you don't know what that idea is yet. One of the reasons you may not be experiencing your highest prosperity already is because you are busy trying to do what someone else told you would make you feel prosperous. Unfortunately, this approach is a lot like getting on a bus that takes you to a destination someone else chose, instead of where you would really like to go. When you get there, you may think it is an interesting place, but you will still feel you need to catch the next bus to get to where you wanted to go in the first place. This is what happens when you let other people dictate your path to prosperity.

You can save yourself a great deal of time if you figure out what you need to do to manifest prosperity and follow that path. This is like getting on a bus that is going to take you where you want to go. For instance, let's say that you have just been offered a promotion with a hefty raise. Everyone you know says you should take it, but you are not sure if you want the increased responsibility because you have been thinking about going to massage school in your spare time.

You could go ahead and take the promotion to please your friends and family. This would take you to a destination of *their* choice. Or you could listen to what you feel would make you truly prosperous and go to a massage school. This would take you to a destination of *your* choice. I'm not saying that massage school is inherently better than the promotion. The important thing is who you let decide your destination.

Of course, your definition of prosperity will change and grow over time. What makes you feel prosperous today may not be what makes you feel prosperous tomorrow. Nonetheless, do not let someone else define prosperity for you. Instead, devote yourself to what makes you feel fulfilled, and you will be prosperous.

WORRYING ABOUT MONEY DOES NOT CREATE PROSPERITY

Worrying about money does not create prosperity. It does the reverse: it creates a lack of money. The more you focus on what you don't have, the less money you will have. I have never seen worrying add even a penny to a bank account, yet so many of us waste so much time doing it. Worrying is really a form of mistrust. Worrying about money is like saying to the Universe,

"I don't trust you to take care of me." Of course, the Universe is no dummy, and will deliver to you exactly what you are really thinking. When you don't trust in the Universe to take care of you, it will bring circumstances into your life to support this belief. Usually, these circumstances aren't very pleasant, and they are almost never very prosperous.

Instead of worrying, try to send out gratitude for everything that you have. Yes, I know that when you have very little it's hard to be grateful, but the more grateful you are, the more you will be able to receive. When you do get money, hold it in your hand and say, "I bless this money, knowing that it will multiply a hundred times over for me and everyone it comes in contact with." Whenever you see a sign that your prosperity is increasing, even a very small sign, acknowledge it with a prayer of thanks. Instead of worrying, be grateful for all your material possessions, your body, your life, the very air that you breathe.

Bless your bills. Hold your bills in your hands and say, "I bless these bills and know that I will be able to pay them easily and effortlessly," or "I bless these bills. I know that as I am sending this money out, even more will come back to fill its place." If you have bills, that is a sign that someone out there trusts in your prosperity enough to extend you credit. This in itself is something to be thankful for.

Remember, if you are constantly going on about how broke you are, all that is going to happen is that you will become more broke. Instead, talk and think about how prosperous you are (even if you aren't there yet, especially if you aren't there yet) and affirm your gratitude for all that there already is in your life.

ALL PROSPERITY IS LIMITLESS AND COMES FROM THE SAME SOURCE

Prosperity is without bounds. There is always enough, and there is nothing that is beyond possibility when it comes to prosperity. Of course, your ability to properly manifest prosperity may be limited if you don't understand its laws, but prosperity itself is unlimited.

Because of this limitlessness, your prosperity can be manifested through any creative vehicle you choose, on any scale you choose. This may come as a surprise to you, especially if you have set limits for yourself about what is and is not possible financially or otherwise. You do not have to work x number of hours or have x number of clients in order to experience true prosperity, nor do you have to do less of what you love and more of what you don't love to become financially successful. Instead, you can experience perfect prosperity, easily and effortlessly, by tuning into Universal Energy.

All prosperity comes from the same source: Universal Energy. This is the energy underlying each and every living thing. Everything is an extension of this energy, including prosperity. Prosperity does not come from money, cars, fancy houses, or any other material object; these are just a few of the ways that prosperity manifests itself. But these are not the source of your good; Universal Energy is the source of all your good.

We sometimes confuse vehicles of prosperity with actual prosperity. Take money, for instance. Some of us devote the majority of our time to accumulating money in the hope that it will help us meet our prosperity goals. But money itself does not bring prosperity; it is simply a vehicle. Any vehicle for prosperity is only as good as the Universal Energy behind it.

Universal Energy is fluid and flexible. It always finds a way to manifest itself to those who are open. Even if you have no idea how you will achieve a goal, Universal Energy will automatically flow to the most appropriate vehicle. You do not have to figure out "how" you are going to achieve something, only what it is that you want to achieve. By staying focused on the final goal rather than the vehicle for the goal, you allow the Universe to fulfill your desire in the smoothest way possible.

Unfortunately, we humans often get hung up on this vehicle issue. It seems that we are always trying to set limits about what is and is not possible with our prosperity, especially when it comes to the appropriate vehicle. I know many people who have some very nice goals, but aren't able to achieve them because they keep focusing on vehicles that aren't working for them, such as unbearable jobs or soul-wrenching relationships.

Of course, there are times when the vehicle is important for us. Say, for instance, that you want to earn a fortune and you want to do it by writing books. Or maybe you want to manifest a new career, but want to make sure it involves helping other people. It's okay to prefer a certain vehicle over another, or one channel over another. After all, prosperity can manifest through any creative vehicle you'd like, on any scale you'd like. But you need to stay open to other possibilities just in case the Universe has a better vehicle in mind.

PROSPERITY COMES FROM BEING OPEN TO UNIVERSAL ABUNDANCE

The Universe is an abundant place. There is more than enough for you and everybody else. Experiencing true prosperity requires only that you acknowledge and be open to receiving this abundance. The more open you are to the idea of abundance, the more prosperity you will manifest for yourself.

Unfortunately, fear can sometimes get in the way of being open to abundance. It seems that all of us have ideas that we need to overcome before we can manifest our highest prosperity. This is the fearful part of us that says, "I'll never be able to make good money doing what I love," or "There is never enough to go around." This is also the part that is secretly afraid of letting go of control long enough for the Universe to do its work. This part wants to keep doing things the same old way, even if that way is not a very prosperous path.

Luckily, you do not have to be trapped by your abundance fears forever. By tapping into your inner courage (which I assure you is ultimately stronger than any fear you have), you can move past these fears one by one. The more you use your inner courage to attempt the things you want to do, no matter how small, the less fear you will have. This is why I encourage people to start working on the small things first—not because you shouldn't be thinking big (you should), but because the small personal victories can sometimes unlock enough inner courage to make several huge leaps forward.

Regardless of your fears, anything is possible when you open yourself up as a creative channel for the Universe. When this happens, you draw upon not only your own energies, but also the energies of the entire Universe. Then you can't help but be prosperous!

EXERCISE:
CREATING YOUR PROSPERITY STORY

Now that you've covered these eight ideas, it's time to do your first prosperity exercise. Go to a private, safe place. Take off your shoes, loosen any tight clothing, get comfortable and relaxed. Begin to breathe deeply and rhythmically. Mentally surround yourself in a bubble of golden-white light. Then begin to tell yourself a story using pictures in your mind. This story is entirely make-believe (for now) and does not need to have any correlation whatsoever to reality as you know it. You can drop your preconceptions of how things "really work" or how things are "supposed to be," since this is just a story.

You are going to tell yourself the story of what it would be like for you to experience absolutely perfect prosperity. Since this is your story, you will have to fill in all the details. Remember that you don't have to worry about what seems possible or what you should be thinking. This is just a story, and it doesn't have to abide by any particular rules or even make sense.

For a moment, try to suspend any negative emotions surrounding prosperity, and create your vision of perfect prosperity. How much money do you have? What kind of work are you doing? How much free time do you have? With whom are you sharing your life? What is your health like?

What kinds of material things do you own? Where are you in your spiritual life? For once, don't worry about what you think you deserve or need. Don't even worry about what is possible. Just take a few minutes to create a picture-story of yourself experiencing perfect prosperity.

Mentally and visually phrase your story as if it is currently taking place. For instance, instead of saying, "I would live in a beautiful two-story Victorian home," say, "I am now living in a beautiful two-story Victorian house." If any doubts creep up, simply say to yourself, "All things are possible through the Divine Spirit within me." Then return to your story. When you feel you finally have completed the story, say a little prayer of thanks to the Universe, acknowledging its ability to manifest your story. End with the affirmation from above: All things are possible through the Divine Spirit within me.

You may want to write down your prosperity story when you are done with this exercise. Practice mentally reviewing your story until you actually believe it is possible. If you like, you can make a tape of your prosperity story and play it back daily. Don't be surprised if your prosperity story starts coming true after a while.

CHAPTER 2

Inflowing Prosperity

Now that you are familiar with the eight principles of prosperity, I'd like to introduce you to another concept: the prosperity cycle.

THE PROSPERITY CYCLE

There is a natural flow to prosperity consisting of both an inflow and an outflow. In order to be truly prosperous, you must maintain a healthy balance between the two.

Understanding how to properly balance the inflow and the outflow is a crucial part of prosperity work. When the two are in balance, your prosperity flows smoothly and abundantly, but when there is too much emphasis on either one, prosperity energy becomes blocked and can't manifest itself in the physical world.

Basically, prosperity cycles in and out of our lives in much the same way that food moves through our bodies. First, we take some in to feed and nourish ourselves, then we eliminate the excess.

Prosperity works the same way. We need to take some in to nourish and uplift ourselves. Then, in order to remain healthy, we must also pass some prosperity out of our lives and along to others.

Of course, what we take in must be greater than what we release. Nonetheless, the two parts of the flow must be nearly equal in order to maintain the cycle. In other words, balancing the inflow and the outflow keeps prosperity flowing the way it should.

In this chapter and the next, we'll cover some specific ways for you to keep your prosperity flowing and balanced. We will start by discussing the inflow, since prosperity always begins here. In chapter 3, we will move into a discussion of the outflow.

THE INFLOW

Energy enters the prosperity cycle through the inflow. On a physical level, inflow is represented by money or material goods; emotional level inflow is love. On a spiritual level, the inflow is the ability to be open to Universal Energy and to have a spiritual understanding.

We start our prosperity work with the inflow, as a healthy inflow is necessary for a healthy outflow. After all, it is difficult to release what you don't have. If you do not have enough time, money, opportunities, or love for yourself, you need to work on your inflow.

UNIVERSAL ENERGY

Regardless of which level of inflow you are interested in, you should start at the spiritual level. Whether we are talking about inflowing money, love, opportunities, or possessions, you always start by learning to be more open to Universal Energy. That's because most imbalances in the inflow ultimately result from not being open to Universal Energy.

When you are open and receptive to Universal Energy in a healthy way, prosperity flows through you and out into your life easily. When you resist the flow of Universal Energy, or try to take more than you can use, prosperity can't properly manifest itself in your life.

Of course, it can be difficult to open up to something you can't see or are not aware of. The following exercise will help increase your awareness of Universal Energy so you can begin to open up to a greater prosperity.

UNIVERSAL ENERGY EXERCISE

Go to a quiet, dimly lit room where you can be alone. Light a candle. Begin to breathe deeply and rhythmically. Close your eyes for a moment, and focus on your breathing. Open your eyes when your breathing becomes relaxed. Relax further by staring deeply into the flame of the candle. With each inhalation, imagine that you are pulling in Universal Energy. Feel the energy moving into every part of your body. Experience yourself completely filled with Universal Energy. Continue breathing this way until your whole being is infused with Universal Energy.

Imagine this Universal Energy transforming into a more specialized kind of energy—prosperity energy. Visualize some of this energy leaving your body and manifesting itself in various physical forms. See all the wonderful gifts and experiences it can give you. Feel the Universal Energy manifesting itself as prosperity. Trust in the energy. Be open to it.

RECEIVING YOUR GOOD

Of course, it's not enough to be open to Universal Energy. This is a start, but it is not the end of your prosperity work. You must also be open to receive your good and to allow others to do the same.

The most common reason many people have problems with prosperity is that they are not open to receive their good.

"I do not feel like I am worthy of prosperity, so I am going to earn my worth by giving all of mine away." Or they are trying to deprive others of their good: "I do not feel like I am good enough to create prosperity, so instead of trying to manifest my own, I am going to take someone else's!"

Both of these ideas are insidious enemies of true prosperity. They pave the way for the two most common problems in receiving: excessive giving and excessive taking. The following section explores these problems in more detail and offers suggestions for becoming truly open to receiving your good.

EXCESSIVE GIVERS AND TAKERS

Many people find it difficult to receive and are always trying to give away too much of their prosperity. This is why they never seem to have enough prosperity or love for themselves. Eventually, they become very drained and bitter about the scarcity in their lives. The only way these people can ever become truly prosperous is to begin to believe they are worthy of prosperity.

Others are so obsessed with receiving that all they ever do is take and take. It seems that they can never get enough, no matter how much they have. They will never be truly prosperous unless they learn how to take only what they need for their own happiness.

Either way, those who have problems receiving have a fundamental problem inside themselves. Deep down inside, they don't believe they are good enough. The prosperity issues they have created for themselves are just an attempt to heal their deeper emotional issues: lack of love and low self-worth.

For instance, excessive givers often feel that they are not good enough, in spite of the fact that others look to them for guidance and support. Rather than dealing directly with their emotional issues, excessive givers attempt to handle them indirectly by sacrificing their personal joy and pleasure to help others. It is as if they believe that if they are able to do enough or sacrifice enough for other people, they will finally be loved by others and will feel okay about themselves. Of course, enough never comes, and they just keep giving and giving until there is nothing left to give.

Deep down inside, excessive takers also believe that they aren't good enough. Unlike excessive givers, takers don't try to earn worth or love by sacrificing their own pleasure. Instead, they try to fill the emotional hole with other people's pleasure and prosperity. They unconsciously believe that if they can find the right people to take care of them and do for them, they will finally feel worthy enough to experience happiness and prosperity. Of course, it doesn't work this way because no one can create prosperity for someone else. Excessive takers just keep taking and taking until there is no one else to take from.

It's no surprise that excessive givers and takers often end up together. The giver provides a seemingly unlimited supply of energy to fill the taker's emotional hole, and the taker seems to have an unlimited ability to receive. The more joy and pleasure the taker is able to leech from the giver, the more the giver tries to prove himself with additional giving until they eventually wear each other out.

Does any of this sound familiar? If it does, it is time to work on being a more balanced receiver. The following sections will help you determine whether you are an excessive taker or giver. After that, we'll end with a meditation to help you become a more balanced receiver, no matter which type you are.

How to Tell If You Are an Excessive Taker

- Are you surrounded by overzealous givers?
- Do you rarely give compliments or gifts to other people?
- Are you quick to complain about others, but easily angered when you are criticized?
- Do you spend so much of your time or money on yourself that you often neglect your obligations to others?
- Do you expect others to do more for you than you are willing to do for them?

- Are you too busy having fun and getting the good stuff to care about how your actions affect other people?
- Do you often refuse to leave a tip or give others the money that is due to them?
- Are you always pushing your obligations off onto other people?

If you answered *no* to most of these questions, skip ahead to the section about givers. If you answered *yes* to more than a few of these questions, you need to balance your receiving with some giving. Practice the following exercises along with the balancing meditation at the end of the chapter.

Receiving Affirmations for Takers

If you have problems trying to create your own good, or if you feel like there is never enough good to go around, practice saying one of the following affirmations several times a day.

I now have more than enough.

I am open to sharing in the blessings of the Universe.

I now take only what I need for my own happiness.

The Universe provides all that I need.

Compliment Other People

If you have had problems with excessive taking, one of the best ways to revitalize your ability to receive is to compliment at least three people a day. Whenever you compliment someone, smile and look into their eyes as if to say "I love you."

If this feels uncomfortable, simply practice smiling at other people. You can also start by practicing your compliments at home in front of the mirror. Later on, you can put a compliment together with a smile and deliver it in person. It really doesn't matter how you learn to do it, just don't forget to compliment other people. Remind others of the good in their lives and the good in yours will increase as well!

Compliment Yourself

Takers also need to learn how to compliment themselves so that they are not always relying on others to do it for them. First, make a list of all of your positive qualities. Run a few copies of this list and post them where you can see them often—in your purse, in the bathroom, on the refrigerator—any place that you frequently visit.

Refer to this list several times a day and give yourself a compliment. Notice that I did not say to ask someone else to compliment you. In order for this exercise to be effective, you have to do it yourself. Any compliment will do, as long as your efforts are sincere. Practice this exercise for at least seven days.

Practice Sharing

If you have always been a taker, try sharing for a change. Take a few minutes a day to imagine yourself doing something good for others or sharing your wealth. Visualize what it would feel like to be a giver instead of a taker. Visualize doing something good for the people who have helped you in the past.

Practice this regularly until you are comfortable with it. When you are ready, start implementing your visualization in the real world by giving to others. You will be amazed at how spiritually and emotionally healing this will be, and how quickly it will get your inflow moving!

Once you have completed these exercises, you can move on to the balancing meditation. Or, if you are curious about the life of an excessive giver, you can read the following section as well.

How to Tell If You Are an Excessive Giver

- Are you mostly surrounded by takers?
- Do you have a difficult time accepting a compliment without giving a lengthy explanation?

- Do you often find yourself refusing tips or money that is owed to you?
- Do you often make excuses for other people's poor behavior?
- Do you feel like you have to be the responsible one while everyone else gets to have fun?
- Do you rarely spend time or money on yourself?
- Do you feel obligated to do more for others than they do for you?
- Do you feel guilty about having or wanting money?

If you answered *yes* to more than a few of these questions, you need to work on being open to receiving. Try the following exercises and practice the balancing meditation at the end of this chapter.

Receiving Affirmations for Givers

If you have problems receiving your good, repeat one of the following affirmations to yourself several times a day.

I am open to receiving.

I am open to all good.

There is plenty for everyone, including me.

I am blessed beyond my wildest dreams.

I deserve prosperity and I claim it now.

I am open to receiving the blessings of the Universe.
I now receive only good.

Compliment Yourself

One of the best ways to help increase your ability to receive prosperity is to compliment yourself. Stand in front of a large mirror and tell yourself that you look wonderful today. Compliment yourself on all of the positive prosperity work you have been doing lately. Compliment yourself on one of your skills or abilities.

Don't worry if doing this exercise feels uncomfortable. It isn't designed to make you feel comfortable, at least not at first. Yet, learning to receive complements from yourself is an important part of opening to prosperity. Practice complimenting yourself a little every day, and soon you will see your prosperity increasing.

Practice Receiving

Visualize yourself receiving all kinds of compliments and gifts from those around you. Then, instead of feeling that you need to refuse the gift or make some lengthy explanation, practice smiling and simply saying one of the following statements: "Thank you! That's wonderful!" "I certainly appreciate this!" "Thanks! I'll put it to good use!"

When you do receive a compliment or gift in real life, use one of the phrases that you have been practicing. Don't try to diminish the power of the gift by trying to refuse it or explain your situation. Accept the good that is offered to you without complaint and without a long speech. Be open to receiving.

And now we move on to the last exercise in the chapter. But first, let me say this: If neither of the above descriptions of givers or takers fit you, pat yourself on the back! You are a healthy receiver! Prosperity is just a matter of time for you.

BALANCING MEDITATION

Practice the following meditation to help you become a well-balanced receiver or whenever you need to increase the flow of your prosperity.

Visualize yourself sitting on a tall golden or silver throne. See yourself dressed in the finest clothes you can imagine, adorned with the finest jewels and accessories. Notice that the room you are sitting in is decorated with beautiful flowers, luxurious rugs, and fine draperies. See yourself sitting upon this throne in a room fit for royalty.

Now imagine scores of people entering this room with smiles on their faces. They are laughing and joking and seem to be having a good time. They have come here today to bring you a gift. Visualize them approaching your throne one by one to offer you gifts. See the wonderful gifts they are offering you—fancy clothes, homes, cars—anything else your heart desires. Imagine yourself gracefully accepting your gifts with a smile and a thanks. Visualize your treasure room overflowing with all the wonderful prosperity that the Universe has brought you. After the people leave, imagine yourself taking some time to really savor your gifts.

Then visualize a different scene. See yourself, still dressed in your finest clothes and accessories, going to visit a friend and offering them a gift. Mentally visit another friend and offer them a gift as well. Continue visiting your friends and loved ones until there are no more left to visit. If you'd like, visit some strangers and imagine yourself offering them gifts as well. Remember, your treasure room is overflowing with prosperity, so you can visit as many people as you'd like.

When you are done doing your giving for the day, mentally return to your throne room to await the next great influx of gifts.

CHAPTER 3

Outflowing Prosperity

We now come to the second part of the prosperity cycle: outflowing. Although many of us come to prosperity work focused on the inflow, we soon realize that the outflow is just as important. In fact, outflowing prosperity in positive, uplifting ways can actually increase your inflow.

SPENDING

Spending is perhaps the most obvious way to outflow prosperity, yet it is the one method that is most likely to be misunderstood. Some people are so addicted to spending that they dig themselves into financial holes; others are such tightwads that no one can stand to be around them. Obviously, neither of these methods supports the healthy flow of prosperity energy.

Spending can be a wonderful way to outflow prosperity into the world when it is done correctly. The following sections explain how you can change your spending habits so that you increase both your inflow and your outflow.

Spend Less Than You Have

The first key to spending correctly is making sure that you always spend less than what you have. This seems obvious, yet there are scores of people who ignore this common sense. In fact, I used to be one of them.

To be fair, it can be very difficult to resist the temptation to spend all that you have or more in our consumer-oriented, credit card pushing society. But when you allow yourself to spend down to your last dime, you are financing today's luxuries with tomorrow's peace of mind. The negative consequences of such an action usually last much longer than any pleasure it gives.

True prosperity comes from living, not spending. Although spending is part of the cycle of prosperity, it is not prosperity. If you want to keep the prosperity flowing well in your life, remember to always spend less than you have.

Spend Lavishly on the Good Stuff

Spend lavishly on the people and things you really enjoy. Do this without hesitation and without apology. Of course, I'm not suggesting you go into debt for the sake of spending. The word "lavish" means different things to different people, and its meaning is certainly dependent upon the amount that they start with. But I am asking you to be generous with yourself.

Make it a priority to spend your money on the things that really uplift you.

I do realize that not everybody has a lot of extra money, but even if you don't have a lot of money, you can still spend a little on yourself. I found this out when I was forced to go on welfare for a year. I had a small child and had just left a defunct marriage even though I had very few marketable skills and a huge pile of debt. To make things worse, I had decided to live with my mother in order to save money, but she suddenly and unexpectedly died.

Needless to say, I was scared and wasn't feeling very prosperous. Yet I always tried to save a little every month, even if it was just five dollars to buy myself a new metaphysical book or a nice piece of chocolate, or to go shopping for "new" clothes at the neighborhood thrift store. The amount wasn't what mattered. What mattered was the fact that I never forgot the true purpose of money—to bring happiness and joy into the world.

Keep in mind that if something is worth buying, it is worth buying well. When you find something you want either for yourself or others, go ahead and get it. Do not cheat yourself by purchasing a cheap substitute that you don't really want. For one thing, it is a waste of good prosperity energy. For another, it doesn't benefit anybody, including the person who sells you the item, for you to be brooding about how you didn't get what you really wanted.

Always make sure to put at least a little money aside for the things that make you happy. Not all of it should go toward the so-called necessities. After all, joy is a necessity too.

Spend Fairly and with a Conscience

Spend your money in a fair way. Always try to pay a reasonable price, and never try to undercut somebody just so you can get a good deal. Your prosperity doesn't come from stealing someone else's prosperity, it comes from getting your life in order so that you can manifest your own prosperity.

Always tip well. Most service people are grossly underpaid and will appreciate your kindness. Even if you are short on cash, you can leave a small thank-you note with your tip. Tipping is a way of honoring another's prosperity energy while increasing your own. On the other hand, when you disrespect another's prosperity, don't be surprised to find your own decreasing!

Don't haggle over prices. This creates a negative energy between you and the seller, and in the long run is disruptive to your prosperity outflow. I do realize that in some situations it is customary to haggle, but make sure that you pay a fair price. You can't be truly prosperous if you are always trying to cheat other people out of their prosperity.

Use your conscience when spending your money. Whenever possible, buy only from those companies and organizations that share your social vision. Don't support those companies that you know are doing terrible things to people or the environment. If no one is left to finance their wrongdoings, sooner or later these companies will have to change their ways. You can be part of that change, which would represent prosperity for the entire human race.

Never buy an item that you feel guilty about purchasing. Instead, ask yourself why you feel that way. Is it because somebody told you that you should feel that way? If so, spend some time getting in touch with your feelings about the matter. Go ahead and buy it if you feel that it is okay, but if you find that there is valid reason for not wanting to purchase that product, don't buy it. It is bad prosperity karma to purchase something you think you really shouldn't—it has a way of disrupting the natural flow of prosperity. Work on the following exercises to get started today on outflowing your prosperity.

Create a Joy Budget
Make a list of all the things that bring you joy. Include your mental, emotional, spiritual, and physical needs. Then set aside a certain amount of money each month to purchase these things.

The first month, you could purchase something that is physically pleasing to you, such as a piece of fine chocolate or a relaxing massage. The next month, you can increase your spiritual joy by getting a psychic reading or purchasing nice candles for your meditation time. After that, buy yourself a bouquet of fresh flowers or an inspirational card to light up your emotional life. Top off your cycle with some mental joy by getting yourself a new book!

Observe Your Joy Purchases

Observe your spending habits carefully for one week. Every time you are getting ready to make a purchase, ask yourself, "Is this something that will bring me joy?" Then note how many times a week you purchase something that brings you joy. Also note the total number of purchases you make in a week. At the end of the week, see how these two numbers compare. If your joy purchases seem low, put some conscious effort into gradually increasing their amount.

I'd like to introduce another important way to keep your prosperity flowing: charity.

CHARITY AND GIVING

Charity is a crucial element of the prosperity outflow. Like spending, charity is often misunderstood. Some people are so charitable that they don't have enough left for their own survival. Others are just the opposite, refusing to share no matter how much they have. Obviously, neither of these actions contributes to a balanced prosperity. Still, charity can be a powerful way to outflow and ultimately increase your prosperity. Let's look at this concept in more detail.

Why Give to Charity?

You may feel that you don't want to give to charity because there is nothing in it for you. The truth is that there *is* something in it for you. Giving to charity keeps your prosperity moving so that more can flow in. Of course, spending also does this, but spending is not a substitute for charity. Charity not only circulates and redistributes prosperity, it also helps demonstrate to the Universe how you would prefer to be treated. If you want the Universe to give freely and charitably to you, you should also give freely and charitably.

There is another reason to give. If prosperity isn't shared, it has a way of turning toxic. This is often the case with people who become wealthy but are stingy. For such people, life is far from joyous. No one wants to be around them, and no one likes them. They don't even like themselves. Instead of being a blessing, money becomes a curse for them. This is what happens when prosperity is not properly outflowed through charity and generosity.

Of course, no one benefits when you are a martyr. The idea isn't to give to the point that you have nothing left for yourself. Giving should in no way negatively affect your emotional or physical comfort; if it does, it's not true charity. But when you share whatever extra you have freely and with love, it will be returned with even greater prosperity!

Give Without Strings Attached

Whenever you give of yourself or your money, don't expect anything in return. True charity means simply giving out of the joy of your heart and sharing the extra that you have with others. It does not mean giving so that you can get a tax write-off or be rewarded by your community. The sharing is your reward. This sharing keeps your prosperity flowing and keeps you free from being burdened with more than you have need for.

Sure, it's tempting to expect a person or an organization to return your gift with a personal favor, but that's not charity—it's networking. In order for charity to be truly effective in raising your prosperity, you have to be motivated by something besides self-interest. Otherwise, you're not sharing your extra, but simply trading it to get more for yourself.

There Are Many Ways to Give

Money is an important form of prosperity energy in our society. One of the highest ways to honor a person or a cause in our society is to give them money. This shows that you really respect and believe in what they stand for. It is one thing to say that you support a cause but it is another thing altogether to hand over your money to it. That is why we have the phrase "put your money where your mouth is."

Just because a person donates money to a cause does not necessarily mean that they wholeheartedly believe in it. Nonetheless, people who wholeheartedly believe in a cause usually donate money to it. Find a person's passion and their purse strings are usually not far behind.

Of course, money is not the only way to give. Giving your time can be just as valuable, if not more so, than giving money. This is especially true regarding generosity toward children. Many children would rather have a little extra love and attention than another fancy toy.

Children aren't the only ones who can benefit from charitable gifts of time. Spouses, parents, siblings, and extended family members all do better when someone cares enough to share a little bit of time with them. So do friends, co-workers, and even pets. Often just taking the time to be together is a more valuable gift than any amount of money!

Giving your talents is another wonderful way to be charitable. No matter who you are, you have a talent that someone else can benefit from. Maybe it's the way you make others laugh, or maybe it's the way you cook. (For that matter, maybe it's the way you make them laugh by the way you cook.) Perhaps you're good at rubbing feet or soothing sore hearts. Maybe you're a good listener, an interesting storyteller. Maybe you're none of these things, but one thing is certain: you are uniquely you. There is no one else exactly like you on the planet, and therefore you have something wonderful to give— yourself.

Now that you understand the rationale for giving, here are some exercises and suggestions to get you started.

Your Giving Plan

Make a list of all the causes that are important to you on a local, national, and international level. Then write out a detailed plan for contributing to these causes with time or money over the next year. Also make a list of other causes you would like to look at in the future. Start carrying out your plan within the next month or so. Review your plan periodically to check your progress.

The Gift of Time

Make a list of all the people who are important to you. Then set aside a time to do something nice with each one of them during the next month. This may be as simple as sharing a phone conversation or taking a walk in the park. A little bit of time and love goes a long ways!

A Gracious Letter

Think of the last time someone did something really nice for you. Sit down and write that person a letter expressing your gratitude and explaining what their actions meant to you and mail the letter.

If you want to be really charitable, make a list of all the people who have been important in your life and send them a short letter thanking them for their help. You will be amazed at how much these letters will mean to people, and at how much it makes them want to help you even more.

Generous Housecleaning

Take a weekend to go through your house examining your possessions. Set aside any things that you are no longer using. Make plans to donate these items to a charity, or to people you know. I do this periodically, and it never fails to get my prosperity moving!

Some Painless Ways to Start Giving

- Instead of spending your change, drop it into a jar. At the end of the month, take the money in the jar and donate it to your favorite charity.
- Set up your bank account so that your charitable contributions are deducted automatically. (Only do this if you have a steady income and can remember to subtract it out of you checkbook.)
- Set aside an hour or two each month to plan your giving strategy for the month.
- Make a list of the favorite people in your life and do something nice for at least one of these people each month.
- Compliment at least one person a day.
- Donate a little bit of time or money to an organization that helped you in the past.
- If you enjoy the arts or music, donate some money to your local art center or public radio station.
- Offer to plant some flowers or clean the office of your favorite charity or the home of a physically challenged neighbor.
- Pick some flowers for the people you care about the most.

- Give an overworked friend a night off from cooking and cleaning.
- Help an elderly neighbor clean her yard or unload her groceries.
- Ask a child what she would like to spend time doing, and then do it with her.
- Cook a meal for a friend or loved one who doesn't get many home-cooked meals.
- Read a book to a child. Better yet, volunteer for thirty minutes a week to help a child learn to read.
- Finally, introduce the idea of giving to people at work and at home. Encourage those who look up to you to be generous in giving also!

One last word on charity…please don't plan on waiting until you are wealthy to share. Most people who have this attitude never get wealthy!

SETTING GOALS

Prosperity work isn't simply about outflowing prosperity. It's also about getting it to outflow into all the right places. This is where goal setting comes in. Setting a goal cuts a channel for Universal Energy and allows your prosperity to manifest in a more concentrated, focused form. A goal gives the Universe something concrete to grab onto, an actual reason to send more prosperity energy pulsing down your pipeline. Trying to outflow prosperity into the physical world without a goal is like trying to drive to another state without a road map. More than likely, you will never get there.

Read on to learn more about goal setting, and how you can use it to get your prosperity properly outflowing.

Goal Setting 101

Many people are intimidated by goal setting. Perhaps it is because focusing on a goal can mean passing up one opportunity in favor of another. For instance, I have chosen to focus my prosperity energy into becoming a metaphysical writer and teacher, but when I was a little girl, I dreamed about becoming a world-famous dancer. No doubt I could have gone that route had I chosen to make dancing my main focus. Instead, I chose to focus on my goals in metaphysics.

Of course, you don't have to marry your goals! Just because you set a goal doesn't mean that you are bound to it for the rest of your life. You are free to choose again at any time. I still believe I could be a world-famous dancer—or anything else I wanted to be. The Universe does not lock us into one path simply because we set some goals!

No matter what goals you choose, goal setting will only work if it is done with joy. If you set a goal simply because it is

51

what you think you should be doing, or because you are trying to please another person, it will not work. Sooner or later you will find that your prosperity cannot flow properly.

The whole purpose of goal setting is to harness the prosperity energy available to you in order to create more joy in your life. Don't look at it as something that you have to do. Instead, look at it as something fun and exciting that you want to do! If you ever get to the point where goal setting makes you stop smiling, you may need to come back to it another day.

Short-term vs. Long-term Goals

Make your long-term goals fantastic. For instance, one of my long-term goals is to be a world-famous metaphysical writer and counselor. Some people would say this goal is unrealistic, but I know that it is possible. When you are setting long-term goals, anything is possible! In fact, the more fantastic your goal, the better!

On the other hand, short-term goals need to be more down-to-earth. One of my short-term goals is to produce one or two books in the next few years. Notice that I didn't say that my short-term goal was to write two books in the next three months. This couldn't be realized. Instead, I have created a short-term goal that I know is feasible. I recommend that you do the same thing with your short-term goals.

Getting Started

The way to get started is simple. Sit down with a pen and paper and write out some goals. If it intimidates you to think too far into the future, set some goals for next week and next month. Later on you can set some more long-term goals. I'd recommend setting at least a one-year and a five-year goal, although you can certainly set your goals for any time frame that you like.

Start in the area that is most important to you. Work on that area for a while. Then when you get that down, set goals for another area. Continue working in this way until you have covered all the areas of importance to you.

Eventually, you may want to try to work on all areas at the same time. This is great as long as you can keep up with it. It's also perfectly acceptable to work on just one or two areas at a time.

Here are some suggestions on areas in which to set goals:

- Finances
- Work
- Creativity
- Pleasure
- Spirituality
- Life mission
- Family

- Love life
- Friendships
- Health
- Education

When You Don't Accomplish a Goal

Inevitably, you will set a goal for yourself that you won't accomplish. When this happens, please don't think this reflects badly upon you. The truth is that it happens to all of us at one time or another. Just because you didn't accomplish a goal doesn't mean that you're a bad person or somehow deficient. Maybe you didn't really want to achieve the goal in the first place. Or perhaps things just got so busy for you that you truly didn't have the time. Maybe the goal you set wasn't realistic for your present life. There are a million possibilities to consider. Don't beat yourself up just because you didn't meet a goal.

CHAPTER 4

Clearing

Prosperity is what happens naturally when you are an open channel for the Universal Abundance. Whenever prosperity doesn't happen, something has gone wrong. Usually this means that you have allowed something to come between you and Universal Abundance. That something is usually nothing more and nothing less than a belief. As countless metaphysicians before me have pointed out, beliefs can be changed. In order to experience perfect prosperity, you will need to confront and release those limiting beliefs.

It really is this simple. If you are willing to release the beliefs that have clogged the prosperity channel, you can experience perfect prosperity. Let's explore some ways to do that.

BASIC CLEARING
First of all, I want you to start by looking back to the prosperity story you created earlier (see page 22). Try to visualize this story. If you didn't write down your prosperity story earlier,

now would be a good time to do so. Remember, your story is about what it would be like for you to experience perfect prosperity. After you have written and reviewed your story, take a moment to reflect on all the reasons why you believe you can't have the things you want in your prosperity story. You can refer to the list as a whole, or you can take each item within your story and reflect on it.

Write whatever comes up without making any judgment. Some of your thoughts may be related to prosperity in general. For instance, you may think, "The reason I can't have prosperity is because no one in my family has ever been prosperous." Or you may think, "I can't ever have too much money because I'd feel guilty." Write these thoughts down.

Other thoughts may be related to more specific prosperity goals. For instance, you may hear yourself thinking, "I can't have that new car because I'll never make enough money." Or, "I can't have a college degree because I'm not smart enough." Write these down, and whatever else comes to mind. Keep writing all the reasons you believe you can't have your highest prosperity until no more reasons come to mind.

I'd like to tell you what I think about the word "can't." As far as I'm concerned, there is really nothing you can't do. "Can't" really means "I choose not to" or "I'm afraid to." Oftentimes, "can't" means "won't" or "shouldn't." But "can't" never really means can't. The fact that you can even think about something shows that it can be done and most likely can be done by you.

Look back over your list of reasons why you "can't" have true prosperity. What do you really mean when you say can't? Do you mean that you are afraid to? Or maybe you mean that you "shouldn't." Perhaps "can't" means that you don't really want to put out the effort. Take some time to review your list and figure out what all your can'ts really mean.

If you'd like, use a separate sheet of paper to rewrite your *can't* sentences to reflect what you are really saying. This will help expedite the cleansing process. For instance, let's pretend that one of your can'ts was "I can't have that much money because I'd feel guilty." You may rewrite it to say something like, "I could have as much money as I want, but other people have told me I should feel guilty if I have more than just a little." Or maybe it really means something like "I am afraid to try to make that much money because I might fail." If you'd like to speed things up a bit, rewrite each one of your sentences in this same manner.

Once you are done deciphering your *can't* list, write Cleared and Released in capital letters across the top of both of your lists. If you like, you can tear up the lists now, for they no longer have any power over you.

Very good. Now we can get down to the next order of business.

RE-WRITING YOUR KARMIC CONTRACT

We all have a karmic contract with the Universe. It is an unwritten agreement between you and the Universe that outlines the situations and lessons you will experience during your time on earth. This contract is usually negotiated before birth. If you are struggling financially or in any other way, more than likely it is because of something you have written into your karmic contract. You may have taken a vow of poverty, suffering, or sickness. Or, you may have simply decided at one point in time that you wanted to know what it was like to struggle. In any case, rewriting your karmic contract can be an important part of clearing.

The karmic contract is a matter of personal choice. I don't pretend to know all the things that you might like to include in your contract. Nonetheless, I've included a sample to help you along. Feel free to use it word for word or change it as you see fit. In particular, you may want to include your specific goals. The main purpose of this exercise is to help you release any attachment to pain and suffering.

A word of caution. Make sure you are ready to experience a new life before you create your karmic contract, because it changes everything. By releasing your attachment to pain and suffering, you allow yourself to start all over again. Believe me, it's wonderful.

The Rewrite

Take a little while to think before you write your new contract. Make some notes about what you would like to include or eliminate. Remember, writing your karmic contract can have a very powerful effect. You should take this exercise seriously. Think carefully and take some time before you begin to rewrite the contract.

Once you are ready to do the rewrite, go to a peaceful place where you can be undisturbed for a while. Get comfortable and try to create an atmosphere appropriate for spiritual work. Light some candles, burn some incense, get grounded and centered, breathe deeply and rhythmically, say a little prayer to invoke your higher power and ask its assistance. You may also want to call upon an archangel or other divine power to assist you.

Continue breathing deeply until you are very relaxed. Then begin to write, choosing your words carefully. If you want to use the sample contract I have provided, make sure you read it thoroughly and agree with everything in it. If it doesn't fit for you, rework it to meet your needs. Either way, performing this exercise will bring you one step closer to true prosperity.

KARMIC CONTRACT

I, _____, am now willing to release all previous vows of poverty, sacrifice, unhappiness, loneliness, sickness, and struggle. Furthermore, I also give up any attachment to suffering or fear of success. I affirm that none of these are qualities of my natural state.

I, _____, now claim my natural right to health, love, happiness, and wealth. I declare that I am now manifesting all my heart's desires, easily and effortlessly, without struggle. I no longer feel the need to create suffering for myself.

I, _____, now affirm that the Universe has been informed of these changes, and it will now begin to respond accordingly. I affirm that I am in an eternal state of perfect prosperity and peace.

This contract nullifies and voids all previous contracts to the contrary.

_____

(Signature and date)

Great! Now that you've rewritten your karmic contract, we can move on to another very important concept.

PHYSICAL CLEARING

Physical clearing is anything you do that allows you body to be relaxed and open to Universal Energy. Basically, this means taking good care of your body and releasing any tension that has been stored in it. Physical clearing is important because your body is your main tool for manifesting prosperity in the physical world.

The condition of you body affects your ability to be prosperous. When your body is feeling light and free, you can manifest all the prosperity you want, but when it is feeling heavy and tense, your ability to manifest prosperity is compromised. That's why it's important to do a little physical clearing every day.

Your body is a storehouse of memories and beliefs from both your heart and mind. Every time you are hurt, annoyed, or angered, your body takes note and files it away. Every time you feel loved and nurtured, your body also takes note and files this away. The body is a sort of cosmic record for all the things that have ever happened to you.

Sometimes your body holds onto hurtful feelings and experiences that need to be released. When this happens, it becomes stiff, weak, tense, or full of aches. Obviously this makes it difficult for you to properly manifest your inner prosperity. That's where physical clearing comes in. Physical clearing allows you to purge your body's record of any past situation which may be preventing you from expressing your highest prosperity. With physical clearing, you can take a hurtful belief or memory that was literally embedded in your body and send it on its way.

One of my favorite ways to clear the physical body is exercise. I try to do a little yoga or walking every day. Of course, these are not the only types of exercise that can help you clear your body. Dancing, jogging, swimming, aerobic exercise, and lifting weights are a few of the many excellent ways to clear it. Nearly any exercise will do, provided it is done on a regular basis and doesn't overstrain the body.

Working with diet is another way some people physically clear themselves. By changing your diet, you can clear your body's memories. My body is at its best when I eat lots of fruits and vegetables and just a little meat. I also like to fast occasionally for a day or two. But each body is different and you have to find the foods that work best for you.

No matter what kind of diet you choose or how often you exercise, you can benefit from spending five minutes a day breathing deeply. It cleanses and revitalizes your internal organs and is one of the best ways to release stress. It also stimulates your body's ability to circulate Universal Energy. It doesn't cost a dime, and you don't need any special instructions. All you need is your own breath and a few undisturbed minutes. If you want to explore this in more detail, there are many good books and classes on the subject.

One of the easiest and most enjoyable ways to physically clear is to get a massage. It requires very little effort on your part and is a wonderfully nurturing experience. Massage not only cleanses your body but leaves you feeling exquisitely relaxed. One of the best things you could ever do for yourself is to get some kind of massage or energy work at least once a month.

Sleep can also be a wonderful way to clear yourself. In fact, it's such a good clearing tool that nature has decreed that we do it every day. Sometimes just a few extra minutes of sleep can make all the difference between feeling frazzled and feeling refreshed. When I am working on a project that proves to be difficult, I sometimes stop and take a short ten- or twenty-minute nap. It seems to sweep away all of my frustrations, and afterward I am able to start fresh with more creativity than before. If you are feeling constantly wornout and stressed, a little extra sleep may be just what you need.

There are many other ways to clear on a physical level: bubble baths, drumming, chanting, and reflexology are just a few examples. Find the ways that work best for you, and practice them regularly.

SPIRITUAL CLEARING

In addition to having a physical body, you also have a non-physical body. This non-physical body is your main tool for receiving prosperity energy from the Universe; therefore, the condition of your non-physical body affects your ability to be prosperous. When it is clear and open, you are able to receive as much prosperity as you like, but when it is dense and heavy, Universal Energy can't make its way in and your ability to receive prosperity is compromised. That's why it's important to practice spiritual clearing on a regular basis.

The non-physical body extends about three feet beyond the physical body. Like your physical body, your aura (another name for the spiritual body) is a storehouse of memories and beliefs, some of them painful. It is even possible to carry painful memories and limiting beliefs from past lives over into this lifetime via your aura. Hurtful feelings or experiences can create tension in the spiritual body, often manifesting as indifference, lethargy, apathy, or downright exhaustion.

An imbalance in the spiritual body can be properly addressed only by spiritual cleansing. Although mental, physical, or emotional cleansing can help, these can't get at the root of the problem. The only way to treat tension in the aura is to remove the hurtful feelings and negative beliefs that have been lodged there.

Energy work heals and realigns the spiritual body. It usually involves laying hands directly upon the body, or working the aura by moving the hands a few inches above the physical body. In either case, Universal Energy is transferred through the sender's hands directly into the receiver's physical and non-physical body.

Whether you practice energy work directly on yourself or have someone else do it for you makes no difference. The effect is the same: tensions in the spiritual body are released and dissolved, and the aura is free to begin to resume its ideal design. Energy work stimulates the non-physical body to heal itself.

There are other ways to spiritually cleanse. I have found that being in nature is one of the simplest yet most effective ways to restore the aura to a pristine condition. It helps to stimulate and revitalize the aura's own energies so that it can cleanse and heal itself. Nature is like food for the aura.

When you are constantly indoors, your spiritual body begins to starve and starts sending you messages to feed it. These messages usually come in the form of fatigue or an existential crisis. Why do you think people who work in offices end up feeling drained and weak, even though their work is not physically demanding? It's because their non-physical bodies are starved for a little bit of nature. On the other hand, many outdoor workers seem to be able to work sunup to sundown and still have energy left to enjoy their evenings. That's because their non-physical bodies have been well fed by their outdoor activities.

You don't have to be an outdoor worker to spiritually cleanse. I have found that a quick walk a few times a week will keep the aura replenished and relatively free of blemishes. I also like to keep several houseplants and fresh flowers around my home as a way of feeding my spiritual body.

Going camping and hiking for a few days is a wonderful way to clear your aura of the gunk that has accumulated. And there's always the option of spending some time outdoors at a park or public garden or in your own backyard. The important thing isn't how you spend your time in nature, but that you do it and you do it often.

Music is another way to spiritually clear. The right kind of music can cut through the spiritual tension. While much of the abrasive stuff nowadays can be downright damaging to your non-physical body, music that sounds ethereal can help cleanse your aura. Visit your local metaphysical bookstore or the New Age section of a music store to find music that will help you.

Certain high-pitched sounds like chimes seem to produce a clear and relaxed aura. Repetitive sounds such as drumming, rattling, chanting, or toning also help. You can buy recordings, or you can purchase instruments to make your own sounds, which can be most powerful.

You don't have to buy a thing to practice chanting or toning. Simply start with a favorite sound or word and repeat it over and over. Do this five minutes a day and you will feel a difference in your aura.

There are many ways to clear on a spiritual level, including salt water, sage, aromatherapy, guided meditation, deep breathing, and prayer. Find the ways that work for you and practice them regularly.

EMOTIONAL CLEARING

The feelings you have about yourself and others can influence your ability to be prosperous. The more you criticize or attack others, the less prosperous you will feel, no matter how much money you have. The more loving and accepting you are, the more prosperous you will feel, no matter how much money you have. This is why emotional clearing is necessary.

Emotional clearing is anything you do that helps release stifled and unpleasant emotions that hold you back from you highest consciousness. Every time you clear, you get rid of a bit of emotional tension, particularly the tension that is blocking you from experiencing prosperity. Emotional clearing helps bring these feelings to the surface so they can be released and dissolved.

What you send out comes back to you. That's why the more love you send to yourself and others, the more prosperous you will become on all levels. This doesn't mean that you need to let someone walk all over you. The question is whether or not you are coming from a loving space.

So often a person annoys us because they remind us of something within us or something from our past. When this is the case, we are not really annoyed by that person so much as we are frustrated with some aspect of ourselves. When this happens, we need to look within and ask ourselves, "What is this situation trying to teach me about myself?"

We all get angry, jealous, or resentful at one time or another. This seems to be part of being human. I'm not recommending that you try to suppress such feelings, because doing so will only make them stronger. Instead, center yourself in a place of love and release these feelings. You can choose to focus on the good in another person and watch your anger, jealousy, or resentment dissolve. Then the floodgates to prosperity will open. Below are some exercises to help you do just that.

RELEASING PAST HURTS

On a piece of paper, preferably pink or light blue, begin to make a list of the people whom you believe have injured you, one by one. Say the name of each person out loud. Then remember why you are so angry with that person. Get in touch with your anger. Feel your pain. Have a box of tissues ready so you can wipe the tears from your eyes.

Allow your suppressed feelings to continue to surface until they are all out in the open. Depending on how in touch you are with your emotional self, this may take several days, or it may only take ten minutes. However, work on only one person at a time. You need to resolve one emotional situation before you go on to the next.

When you are done releasing your feelings, make a list of all the things that you once loved about that person. It does not have to be a long list; it is just something to help remind you of that person's good qualities. Think of what attracted you to that person in the first place, or if it is a family member, think of your happiest memories with them. Take a moment to write down some of their best qualities.

You can complete your emotional release and healing by saying, "I forgive you, and I release you to the love of God/dess." Then move on to the next person on your list. Do not do more than you can handle. If this starts to be too intense for you, put your list away and come back to it later.

CLEARING AND BLESSING EXERCISE

This exercise is best for releasing emotions which originated more recently. Try to remember the last time you felt jealous, critical, angry, or resentful toward another person. Bring that person's picture up in your mind. Speak their name aloud. Then mentally say to that person, "I now forgive you for _____. I release you from my jealousy (or anger, resentment, etc.). I bless you and all the good within you. I now affirm that both you and I are perfect, whole, and complete, and we are one within the mind of God/dess."

Repeat this exercise every time you feel yourself experiencing jealousy, anger, criticism, resentment, or envy, or whenever someone annoys you, no matter how slight the experience. This exercise can also be done any time you are feeling annoyed with yourself; simply insert your own name into the exercise.

If you really want to manifest prosperity, then do as Jesus says: love your enemy. Use the above exercise to send out love energy to you worst enemy, or to anyone who has ever made you extremely angry. Better yet, try doing something nice for this other person. You will be amazed at the improvement in your prosperity!

Practice the exercises in this section as often as you need to. Over time, you will create your own clearing exercises. That is good. There are many ways to clear besides the ones I have presented here. Singing, writing, and gardening are some other things I do to clear myself. Find the ways that work best for you and do a little bit of clearing every day, especially before you go to bed at night and when you get up in the morning.

CHAPTER 5

Transforming Your Poverty Patterns

Congratulations—now you've worked through your "can'ts" and rewritten your karmic contract! Hopefully, you've also practiced some emotional and physical clearing. Before we go any further, I'd like to share with you some things I have learned about how the Universe works.

- There are no true "accidents."
- Everything that is happening to you now is happening for a reason.
- Everything that is happening now is an attempt to fulfill a "need" within you.
- Therefore, if you want to change something about your life, you must first figure out what you are trying to gain from it.

For instance, if you are experiencing poverty, on some level you must feel a need for poverty. If you are experiencing frustration in your career, on some level you must feel a need for frustration. If you are experiencing melodrama in your love life, on some level you must feel a need for melodrama.

Does it make you feel angry to hear me say these things? Good. That means we are getting somewhere. You really don't have to "need" poverty, frustration, or melodrama—no more than you have to "need" a twenty-pound rock dropped on your foot. You would still live if you removed poverty, frustration, or melodrama from your life. Indeed, there are some soul-crushing costs inherent in these patterns.

And yet, like so many other people, you continue to hold onto these patterns or similar ones. Why? It is certainly not because you like these experiences. There is not much to like about them. Nor is it because these experiences are necessary. The Universe does not require that you suffer or struggle in order to experience true prosperity. Yet you keep holding onto these patterns because they are basically an attempt to fulfill a real or perceived need that you have.

In other words, if you are struggling financially, it's obvious you aren't enjoying it. But there must be some payoff: you must think the financial struggle is doing something for you. Let me give you an example from my own life. I grew up in a poor family. I always thought that my finances would get better as soon as I left home. However, a few years after I left home, things only got worse. In spite of the fact that I was hardworking, intelligent, and creative, it seemed I could never get ahead.

Why? I pondered the question and found the answer. I was afraid that my friends and family wouldn't like me anymore if I made "too much" money or was "too successful." After all, they didn't seem to like anyone who had more than they did. Struggling financially like most of the other people I knew was a way that I could finally "fit." I had never fit as a child in my family. At the very least, I knew I wouldn't offend anybody if I continued to be poor. In other words, I was hanging on to my poverty as a way of gaining the approval of my childhood friends and family.

My story is not unique. You probably have had your own pattern that you've held onto in order to try to meet some need. Most of us have several of these patterns. These patterns (and others like them) stand in the way of perfect prosperity. That's why I call them poverty patterns. While such patterns are usually an attempt to fulfill real or perceived needs, they always leave us feeling empty inside.

One of the most remarkable things you can do for yourself is discover what your main poverty pattern is, then free yourself of it. Of course, if you want to be truly free, you will need to identify what it is you are getting out of your poverty pattern. Then you must find a more appropriate way to meet this need, or in some instances, be willing to release the need altogether.

My need to gain the approval of my old friends and family was keeping me poor until I decided I didn't really need their approval after all. Sure I loved them and wanted to get along with them, but it became more important to focus on achieving my highest goal. Ironically, they seemed to approve of me more once I made this decision.

Of course, some needs we are trying to meet with our poverty patterns are legitimate. For example, if you have a lot of melodrama in your love life or your finances, you may discover that you are simply trying to make your life a little more exciting. There is nothing wrong or unhealthy about that, but surely you can find other ways to create some excitement besides these painful relationships or unpredictable finances.

If you are ready to free yourself from your poverty patterns, please complete the following exercise.

IDENTIFYING POVERTY PATTERNS

Make a list of all the things that are happening in your life right now that you're not quite happy about. Use the "Releasing Poverty Patterns" worksheet at the end of this chapter if you like. Feel free to include anything that is bothering you, regardless of whether it relates directly to money or not. For instance, your list may look something like this:

- I have just enough money to get by.
- I am constantly being passed over for promotions and raises.
- All my lovers leave me for someone else.
- I am always sick.

After you are done listing your poverty patterns, take a good long look at each one. For each item on your list, ask, "What am I trying to get out of this?" For instance, if you are struggling financially, ask what you get out of financial struggle. Does it make you feel noble? Does it give you an excuse not to do what you love? Or maybe it keeps you from worrying about other people's opinion of you? Maybe it's a combination of all of these.

Go through each item on your list this way in an attempt to find out what possible benefit may be coming from each one, what need each item is attempting to fill. Or if you'd like, work on just one poverty pattern at a time. Either way is fine. Give yourself plenty of time to complete this part of the exercise.

When you're finished, fill in the worksheet where it asks what needs you are attempting to fulfill. Keep in mind that some poverty patterns may have several benefits. For your convenience, I have included a list of possible reasons why you may be holding onto a poverty pattern.

You could be holding onto a poverty pattern because:

- It makes you feel special.
- It keeps you from having to do what you are afraid to do.
- Other people are sympathetic.
- Other people admire your martyrdom and struggle.
- It's a way of trying to gain someone's approval.
- It's a way to recreate your childhood or something that is familiar to you.
- You are secretly afraid of success.
- You want to avoid the real issue.
- It keeps you from having to do things for yourself.
- It gives you the feeling that you are in control.
- Someone told you this is the way you are, and you don't want to upset them.
- It keeps you from having to assert yourself.
- It gives you a sense of excitement.
- You think it is noble to suffer this way.
- It keeps you safe from intimacy.

There are many more reasons for holding onto poverty patterns. Why are you holding onto yours?

CREATING PROSPERITY HABITS

Now that you've identified your poverty patterns and what you might be getting out of them, it's time to replace them with prosperity habits, new patterns you can design for yourself that can increase your prosperity.

First, take a moment to review what needs you are trying to meet with your poverty patterns. Look at each one in turn and ask yourself whether there is a better way to accomplish this objective. For instance, let's say that you have discovered that unpredictable and chaotic finances are a way for you to get some excitement in your life. A better way to meet this need may be to travel, to participate in daredevil sports, or to begin to do the things you have always wanted to do, but have never tried. The new plan that you come up with is a prosperity habit instead of a poverty pattern.

Maybe the need you are attempting to fulfill isn't really a need at all, and it's time to give up the desire for that experience. For example, you may discover that you have been holding on to your poverty pattern because you enjoy the sympathy that you receive from other people. This is sometimes the case when people choose to stay in unbearable relationships or jobs. In this instance, your new prosperity habit should involve looking for a way to move beyond the need rather than looking for a new way to feed the need. Instead of seeking sympathy, perhaps you can focus on being more assertive or investing in relationships that nurture you.

Take a minute to see why you have been holding on to your poverty patterns. Ponder how you could do things differently. Come up with a new way of doing things, a way that leads to prosperity instead of poverty. Be creative. There is always more than one way to do something, and if it truly needs to be done, the Universe will help you find a way that is helpful and uplifting. If you like, write your new strategies on the "Releasing Poverty Patterns Worksheet."

In case you are wondering, the prosperity habits I proposed for myself were to focus more on self-approval and being my highest self, regardless of what others thought. By staying focused on these habits instead of my old poverty pattern, I have been able to increase my prosperity on all levels.

If you like, you can make a master list of your new prosperity habits. Hang it where you can see it often. Make sure you review the list at least once a month. Reward yourself whenever you feel you are doing well, and be gentle when you feel yourself slipping back into your old patterns. Remember that change takes time.

WAYS TO REINFORCE
YOUR PROSPERITY HABITS

After you have come up with ideas for replacing your poverty patterns with prosperity habits, you can create affirmations to help remind you of your new prosperity habits. Affirmations are positive statements that you say over and over to yourself. For instance, if you had been trying to create excitement by having unpredictable finances, you might repeat to yourself, "I now choose to do the things that are really exciting," or "My life is naturally exciting," or even "It's exciting to have stable finances."

Or, if you are trying to focus on assertiveness instead of wanting sympathy, you might say, "I am open and assertive, easily and effortlessly," or "I now have positive ways of receiving attention from others." Be creative and come up with affirmations that fit your unique situation. See chapter 7 for more information on prosperity affirmations.

Symbolic acts and magic are also powerful tools for reinforcing prosperity habits. Perform a prosperity spell or ceremony to announce your new prosperity habits to the world. Write your prosperity habits on a small slip of paper, put them in a bottom of a flowerpot, and plant flowers over them to symbolize your new growth. Draw a picture of yourself enacting your prosperity habits. All magic and symbolic acts serve to enlist the help of your unconscious mind in achieving your desire, so be creative and find the symbolic act that is right for your prosperity habits. See chapter 8 for more information on prosperity magic.

Remember that prosperity habits only work if they are truly habits. You have to make them part of your life. Your prosperity experience will only change when you change. That's why I encourage you to begin living your prosperity habits today.

RELEASING POVERTY PATTERNS WORKSHEET

Poverty Patterns:

The "Needs" I Am Attempting to Fulfill:

New Prosperity Habits:

CHAPTER 6

Prosperity Means Valuing Yourself

Now that we have poverty patterns out of the way, I'd like to share with you more ideas that will help you to become prosperous.

YOU ARE WORTHY

To the extent that you believe this, you will be able to manifest prosperity in your life. No matter what you have been told in the past, you are worthy of prosperity, love, health—anything you desire. No matter who you are or what you have done, you are a holy child of the Universe. As such, you are valuable and inherently worthy. You do not need to do anything to gain worth.

What do you think of when you hear these words? Do you think, "Yes! That's right"? Or do you hear yourself thinking, "No, I'm worthless"? What does your body do when it hears these words? Do you feel yourself smiling or nodding? Or do you feel your stomach tying itself in knots? The more resistance you have to this idea, the more important it is for you to integrate it into your consciousness.

To experience prosperity, you must first believe that you are worthy! Otherwise, all the prosperity magic and meditations in the world will do nothing for you. I have known many bright people who ended up feeling unsuccessful, in spite of great talent and strong backgrounds. What they all seemed to have in common was one thing: low self-worth. Deep down inside, they did not believe that they were worthy. Because of this core belief, they found it difficult to experience true success or prosperity.

You are no different. If deep down you don't believe you are worthy, you will not experience true prosperity, but if you acknowledge and accept your own worth, prosperity will begin to manifest in your life, easily and effortlessly.

Unfortunately, many of us were not raised to believe we are worthy. Perhaps as a child you were belittled by the people and institutions around you. Or maybe you simply didn't have any positive role models to teach you how to value yourself. Many of us struggle with prosperity issues because of these very reasons. Nonetheless, it is not too late to learn to value yourself and to open up to greater and greater levels of prosperity!

BECAUSE YOU ARE WORTHY, YOU DESERVE ONLY THE BEST

There is no need for you to settle for second best. The Universe wants you to have your greatest desires, and that is what you deserve.

YOU WILL ALWAYS BE WORTHY

No matter what you have done or haven't done you will always be an inherently worthy part of the Universe. Your worth can never be lost and you will always be deserving of true prosperity.

Maybe you have made some mistakes in your life. Perhaps you have even done some things that you feel were terribly wrong. Nonetheless, your inherent worth can never be taken away. No matter what you have or haven't done, you are still as valuable to the Universe as the day you were created. Worth is something bestowed by the Divine Presence. It can't be altered or affected by mere human action. When you feel you've messed up in life or have done something bad, you're still worthy. Regardless of your actions, there is never a need to regain your worth. You have always been worthy of true prosperity and always will be.

YOU DO NOT NEED TO DO ANYTHING
TO GAIN WORTH

There is a lot of talk these days about "gaining" self-worth, but as I pointed out earlier, you don't need to do anything to gain worth. You already have it. In fact, you are so worthy that the Universe would be incomplete without you. You may have been fooled into believing that you have to do something in order to be considered worthy. This simply isn't true. Your worth is not dependent upon being perfect or even being good. Remember, your actions do not give you worth, the Universe does.

Many people look to relationships or money to bring them self-worth. They believe that if they could only make a certain amount of money or meet the right person, they would feel worthy. Luckily, the Universe doesn't work this way. Self-worth doesn't come from money or relationships. Like all good things, it comes from Universal Energy—the energy that you are made of.

There is no "right" amount of money or "right" relationship that is going to convince you of your self-worth. You have to convince yourself. In fact, as long as you feel that you are un-worthy, you are not going to attract the "right" person or the "right" amount of money. Instead, you will attract people who, like you, think that you are unworthy, or you are going to get just enough money to reinforce the idea that you're not good enough.

Some people think that worth can be earned through good deeds. It's nice to have good deeds in the world, but self-worth can't be "earned" any more than it can be bought. There is no need to earn worth; it is already within you. Besides, the best good deeds are the ones where the person isn't trying to "earn" anything. Whether or not you are a do-gooder, you are worthy and deserving of prosperity.

YOU MUST BELIEVE YOU ARE WORTHY TO RECEIVE GOOD

In order to receive the good of the Universe, you must believe that you are worthy of it. When you are feeling good about yourself, prosperity flows through you and manifests in your life easily, but when you feel you are unworthy and undeserving, true prosperity simply can't make its way into your life.

Prosperity operates on the law of attraction. The more you value yourself, the more you are able to attract the things and experiences that are of value to you. When you do not value yourself, it is difficult to attract the things into your life that you desire. That's why perfect prosperity always involves acknowledging your self-worth and value.

If you don't believe you are worthy, you can't take full advantage of your potential blessings. Believing that you are not worthy is like saying to the Universe, "Send the good stuff somewhere else. I don't deserve it." On the other hand, believing that you are worthy is like saying to the Universe, "Yes! Send the good stuff here. I deserve it."

Your highest prosperity will manifest only when you become totally and truly aware of your inner worth. Of course, most of us appreciate our self-worth only to a degree. That's why we are only somewhat prosperous. By learning to really appreciate your self-worth, you can become an open channel for prosperity.

To take the next step in claiming your true prosperity, work the following exercises.

SELF-WORTH INVENTORY

Write the words "Self-Worth Inventory" at the top of a blank sheet of paper. Begin to make a list of all the good things about yourself. Include your personality traits and your positive physical characteristics as well as your talents and skills. Record any of your important accomplishments, even if you think they are important only to you. Here is a short sample of what a self-worth inventory may look like:

Sample Self-Worth Inventory

- I learned to tie my shoes when I was six years old.
- I wrote my first poem when I was ten.
- I make the best salads.
- I have beautiful eyes.
- I am loving and kind.
- I have written and published several articles.
- I was the first one in my family to go to college.

Since this is an important document, make your list as thorough and exhaustive as possible. Write it down on good paper or card stock. Keep in mind that you don't have to limit yourself to a few things or even to the present moment in your life. Write down whatever comes to mind, no matter how trivial or off-the-wall it may seem.

Review your self-worth inventory often, especially any time you catch yourself doubting your own worth. If you really want to get your prosperity flowing, read your inventory daily for a few weeks or even a few months. By focusing on the expressions of your self-worth, you will increase your prosperity many times over. Be sure to add to your prosperity inventory as often as you'd like.

CREATING A VALUE LIST

At the top of a sheet of paper, write the words, "I value myself, therefore." Now, repeat that statement to yourself out loud, "I value myself, therefore," and write down anything that comes to mind. For example, you may write, "I value myself, therefore I always give myself time to meditate," or "I value myself, therefore I make art." Write down everything that comes to mind until you can't think of anything else. Don't worry about how good your list sounds, or whether or not it makes sense. The important thing is to keep writing until you run out of ideas. If you need to, use additional sheets of paper.

Take the time to read this list at least once a day for several days, until you feel you have begun to truly act as if you value yourself. Try to do at least one thing from your list every day. Of course, the more you work on realizing your self-worth, the more you will have to add to your value list, so make sure that you update it often. Whenever you are feeling down, pull this list out and read it again. It will remind you of what you need to do to show yourself that you are truly valued.

SELF-WORTH AFFIRMATIONS

In addition to your self-worth inventory and your value list, you may want to do some affirmations of your self-worth. Stand in front of a large mirror and look deeply into your own eyes. Say, "I am worthy." Repeat this statement a few times. Notice how your body feels when you say this, notice what thoughts are going on in your head. Continue to repeat "I am worthy" for another minute or two.

If you experience any resistance whatsoever during this time, you need to step up your affirmations. Tell yourself at least one hundred times a day statements like "I am worthy," "I am deserving," "I am entitled to good," and so forth. When you are able to say these without reservation, move on to a prosperity variation of the same statements. For instance, you could practice saying to yourself, "I am worthy of true prosperity," or "I am deserving of prosperity." The more you practice these affirmations, the more prosperous you will become on all levels.

YOU DESERVE ONLY THE BEST!

In whatever you do, you deserve to have everything first-class. What do you think of when you hear those words? Do you think, "Yes! That's right"? Or do you find yourself thinking, "I don't deserve to have anything first class"? What does your body do? Do you feel yourself smiling? Or is your jaw clenching? The more resistance you have to this idea, the more important it is that you integrate it into your consciousness.

So many of us create scarcity by automatically expecting and claiming only mediocre things for ourselves. Instead of seeing ourselves as the CEO or chairperson, we see ourselves as the low woman or man on the totem pole. Instead of asking for another ten or twenty thousand or more dollars a year, we ask for just enough to get by. With this kind of limited thinking, it is no wonder we aren't operating at our most prosperous level.

We can all have our heart's desire. In fact, that is exactly what the Universe has intended for us. But if we expect to just get by, that will be our experience. The Universe is like a restaurant. What you order is what you get. If you choose to order ground round even though you could have prime rib, ground round is what you will get.

I have known many wonderful, talented people who ended up in second-rate relationships, unsatisfying jobs, and unhappy lives. What they all seemed to have in common was this: Deep down inside, none of them believed that they deserved the best. Because of this, they were unable to create true prosperity for themselves. You are no different. If deep down inside you do not believe that you deserve the best, you will experience only second-rate prosperity.

Fortunately, it does not have to be this way. Even if you have only had second-rate experiences in the past, begin to expect that you will now live first-class, whether we are talking about jobs, money, health, relationships, or even spirituality. When you decide that you are no longer going to accept second best, the Universe delivers the best for you. Instead of waiting around for the Universe's leftovers, you can claim the best for yourself.

If you are struggling financially, stop focusing on pennies. Instead, be open to receiving large bills. Ask for enough to be comfortable, not just for what you need. If you are having problems with relationships, focus on manifesting an ideal relationship. Don't just accept the next person who comes along. If health is your concern, be open to receiving the best healing you could possibly imagine. You deserve to do more than just get by. Expect and ask for the very best—you will receive it!

When you're ready to start claiming a first-class life for yourself, do the following exercises.

RESTAURANT EXERCISE

Go into your favorite restaurant and order the most expensive item on the menu that seems appetizing. Don't order a substitute just because it's a few dollars cheaper. Include dessert and wine or a nice non-alcoholic drink with your order. Right before you pay for your first-class dinner, mentally or verbally affirm to yourself, "I deserve only the best and that is what the Universe gives me." Then imagine yourself receiving all the best things and experiences that you desire. Know that it will be so. Practice this exercise every time you go to a restaurant and practice it every time you go shopping or buy an article of clothing. When you find something you want, make sure you get it, even if it's a few dollars more than you usually pay. After all, you're worth it!

DRESS IN YOUR BEST

Here is another way to gently push yourself toward accepting the best. Set aside a few hours to go through your wardrobe. Look carefully for any clothes that are badly stained or torn, and keep your eyes open for items that aren't comfortable, or simply aren't you anymore. Set aside whatever you don't want and get rid of these as soon as possible. Go out and buy yourself something new, something that looks good on you right now, not what will look good next year or what might have looked good last year. After all, you do deserve the very best.

PROSPERITY EQUALS SELF-LOVE

All prosperity is a form of self-love. The more you love yourself, the more prosperous you will become on all levels. The more you love yourself, the more money will flow into your life easily and effortlessly.

Both money and true prosperity come naturally when you allow yourself to be an open channel for Universal Energy. Unfortunately, self-hate (even the tiniest bit) closes down the channel and alienates you from your connection with all living things. That is why you must learn to love yourself if you want to create prosperity. Without self-love, you won't be able to access the Universal Energy necessary for perfect prosperity.

Some people are afraid that if they love themselves they are being selfish. True self-love has nothing to do with being selfish. Nor does it have anything to do with arrogance or vanity; these are really forms of self-hate. Instead, true self-love means getting in touch with the Divine Spirit within you. Being in touch with this makes it difficult to even conceive of being selfish because loving yourself allows you to be spirit-centered instead of ego-centered. And when you are spirit-centered, you can't help but be prosperous!

On the other hand, when you are constantly criticizing yourself consciously or unconsciously, you will find it difficult to manifest prosperity. When you are devoting your energy to acts of self-hate and self-destruction, no matter how small, you will find that you cannot achieve true prosperity, no matter how much money you have.

The Universe mirrors back your thoughts about yourself. If you think loving and gentle thoughts about yourself, you will receive back a loving and gentle reality. If your thoughts about yourself are fierce, judgmental, and filled with self-hate, you will receive back a reality that affirms these thoughts. That's why you can never experience true prosperity without first loving yourself. The exercises below are designed to help you do just that.

SELF-LOVE AFFIRMATIONS

Sit down in front of a mirror, or hold up a hand mirror. Staring deeply into your own eyes, say out loud, "I love myself." Repeat this statement a few times. Notice how your body feels when you say this, what thoughts are going on in your head. Continue to repeat "I love myself" for another minute or two.

If you experience any discomfort or resistance, you need to work a little on these affirmations. Practice saying things like "I accept myself," "I approve of myself," and "I honor myself" fifty to a hundred times a day. This may seem like a lot, but it will probably take you less than ten minutes. Do these affirmations daily, preferably in front of a mirror, until you are comfortable with them. After a while, you can try saying the words with your eyes closed and your hands either embracing your face in a face hug, or wrapped loosely around your body in a full-body hug. Because a hug is a universal symbol of love, when you are able to hug yourself without feeling shame, you know that you truly do love yourself.

If you like, you can add a prosperity variation to your self-love affirmations. For instance, after you are very comfortable saying I love myself, change the words to "I love myself, therefore I am prosperous." Continue practicing these affirmations until you can virtually do them in your sleep, and watch your prosperity grow.

SELF-LOVE MONEY JAR

Decorate a plastic or glass jar with your favorite colors and symbols. Write "Self-Love Jar" on the outside of the jar. Every time you catch yourself criticizing or saying something bad about yourself, put in a specified amount of money. If you don't have enough money at the time to do so, write down the amount of your "self-love debt" on a piece of paper, and put it in the jar. Deposit the money you owe in the jar as soon as you get paid. At the end of the week, use the money in the jar to buy or do something that really makes you feel special. If you really want to accelerate the prosperity process, you can also make deposits in your self-love jar every time you catch yourself saying or doing something good for yourself. Please note that the amount of money doesn't matter; what does matter is being consistent about using the jar.

SELF-LOVE/PROSPERITY PICTURE

Take the largest picture you have of yourself and paste it on a sheet of white cardboard. All around the picture, write positive statements of self-love, such as "I love myself" and "I value myself" or "I am worthy," or any other positive statement that comes to mind. At the bottom of the picture, in big letters, write the words, "I deserve the best." Also, feel free to draw or use stickers on your picture to symbolize prosperity and self-love. When you are done, hang your prosperity picture where you can see it every day.

CHAPTER 7

Prosperity Talk 101

The more you talk about something, the more powerful it becomes. The more you think and talk about something, the more you will have of that something. The level of prosperity you have now is directly related to the words you have used in the past. In this section you will learn how to change your language in order to manifest your inner prosperity in the outer world.

THE BASICS

Watch what you say and don't say to others and to yourself. When we are struggling with prosperity, we often feel like victims with no control of our lives. However, there is one thing you always can control: your language. You can choose words that create either prosperity or scarcity. When you say, "I am broke," the statement itself creates poverty. When you choose to say to yourself, "I am prosperous and successful," you create prosperity. Obviously, this statement may not feel true. That doesn't matter. It is true inside of you, for you already have unlimited inner prosperity, and by speaking words that honor and acknowledge your inner prosperity, you make it true in a literal sense.

You will find it easy to use prosperity talk on a daily basis. Simply tell yourself every day how prosperous you are, how easily money flows to you, and how effortlessly you achieve success. Every day, remind yourself that you are connected to the Universal Energy, and that all prosperity comes from this Universal Energy. Every day, affirm prosperity to yourself, especially if you feel you have not achieved it yet. By thinking and talking about prosperity, you will create it.

Any time you hear yourself say something that reinforces scarcity (financial or otherwise), try to counter it with words that reinforce your natural abundance. For instance, if you hear yourself say, "I don't have enough money to..." immediately catch yourself and say, "I now have more than enough money to...." Instead of saying, "I never have enough money to pay the bills," say, "I always have more than enough money to pay the bills." Or if you find yourself saying, "I'll never be able to afford...." claim your prosperity by stating aloud, "I am now enjoying...."

You may not always catch yourself before you make a statement that is dangerous to your prosperity. That's okay; you don't have to be perfect to practice prosperity talk. Just make sure that you practice some prosperity talk as soon as you realize you've said the wrong thing. For instance, if you realize that fifteen minutes ago you were going on and on about your money problems, try to take five minutes to look in the mirror and tell yourself how much your inner prosperity is manifesting itself more and more every day. Or take a moment to affirm to yourself that you now have plenty of money.

Of course, all of us occasionally make such mistakes. Some of us do it on a regular basis. Fortunately, you can undo the damage by following it with prosperity talk.

PROSPERITY AFFIRMATIONS

If you want to bring prosperity talk to its highest level, use prosperity affirmations.

Choose one or more from the list below, or create your own to fit your situation, and repeat it at least fifty to a hundred times a day.

Prosperity Affirmations

I have plenty of money, easily and effortlessly.

I am prosperous and fulfilled.

I deserve prosperity and I claim it now.

Money and success come to me easily.

I am a magnet for Divine Prosperity.

I make plenty of money just doing what I love.

I am a channel for Universal Prosperity.

It is safe to be prosperous.

Money flows to me from all directions, easily and effortlessly.

All that I need is given to me before I even ask.

I have all that I desire, easily and effortlessly.

There is plenty for everyone, including me.

I am worthy.

I can have it all.

I am good enough.

My financial situation is wonderful.

I have plenty of opportunities.

My life is filled with prosperity on all levels.

I now have _____ (whatever you desire).

_____ comes to me easily and effortlessly.

REFINING YOUR PROSPERITY TALK

You will notice that many of these affirmations begin with the words "I am" and "I have." That's no accident. Every time you say "I am" or "I have," you are affecting your prosperity profoundly, for better or for worse. Whatever comes out of your mouth after those words is what you are choosing to be true for you. Sometimes we make such statements carelessly without thinking: "I am broke," "I am fat," "I have too many bills," "I have an ugly body," "I am stupid," "I am sick," "I am in a terrible relationship," "I am desperate and lonely." Are these really the things you want for yourself? Of course not! And yet if you say such things, this is exactly what you will have.

Think of it this way: whenever your unconscious mind hears the words "I am" or "I have," it is as though it has received a command from you. If you tell yourself "I am broke," your mind quickly sets about making that statement true. If, on the other hand, you tell yourself, "I am wealthy and prosperous," your mind will quickly set out to make this statement true. Your mind, being part of the One Mind and the Universal Consciousness, is a very powerful tool and can make anything happen, for better or for worse.

No matter what happened in the past or what you have been told, you do not have to claim words like "broke," "poor," "fat," "ugly," "sick," or "stupid" for yourself. Instead, you can use words like "prosperous," "energetic," "beautiful, "or "lovable" to create the reality that you really want for yourself.

The same is true of "I have." You can choose to follow "I have" with phrases that will make you more prosperous, such as "plenty of money," "a bulging bank account," "a wonderful relationship," or "a fulfilling career." By doing so, you will increase both your prosperity and the quality of your life many times over.

SUSPECT PHRASES

There are two phrases you should avoid if you want to achieve your highest prosperity: "When I have enough money," or "When I have enough time." A few years ago I found myself wishing I could have a massage once a week, but it seemed impossible because I didn't have the money. I kept saying to myself, "When I get enough money, I am going to have a massage once a week," but after two years, I was still scraping by with a few massages a year. I kept wondering, "Why isn't this happening for me?" After all, I was practicing prosperity talk, wasn't I?

Shortly after, I told a friend about my plan to get a weekly massage once I had enough money. He pointed out that I didn't need a lot of money to get a massage once a week. He suggested that if I stopped focusing on having "enough money" and started focusing on having my weekly massage—however that would come into being—weekly massages would start happening.

I chose to drop the words "when I have enough money" from my vocabulary altogether and I started saying, "I am getting at least one massage a week" and "I am able to get a massage as often as I like." In a few months, I started getting my weekly massages and loved every minute of it. I didn't have to win the lottery to accomplish it. My income was about the same; through a combination of trades and a student discount, I was able to get all the massages I wanted.

The same idea can be applied to your life. No matter what you situation is, there is no need for you to say, "When I have enough money." When you say this, you are keeping your goal somewhere out in the future, forever dangling in front of you. If you want prosperity, substitute the words "I now have" or "I am now able to" for "When I have enough money." For example, when you say, "When I have enough money, I am going to go to Hawaii," fix it by saying, "I am now able to take a wonderful Hawaiian vacation." Or if you hear yourself say, "When I have enough money, I am going to buy a new car," try saying "I now have a beautiful new car."

Remember, you do not have to wait until you have enough money to realize your desires. Money is just one of the many vehicles the Universe uses to bring prosperity. Discarding the phrase "when I have enough money" allows you to be open to receive your desire in other ways.

Before I started doing my prosperity work, I must have said "when I have enough time" at least a half a dozen times a day.

The sad thing is that when most of us use this phrase, it usually refers to something very important to our soul purpose. You don't believe me? Listen to the statements I have heard people make frequently. "When I have enough time, I will be a writer." "When I have enough time, I will be an artist." "When I have enough time, I will meditate." "When I have enough time, I will go back to school." "When I have enough time, I will spend more time with my children."

It's funny. You rarely hear people saying, "When I have enough time, I will do the laundry," or "When I have enough time, I am going to play some computer games." Almost always they follow it with something important. When you make such a statement, it is often a curse of death for the things that are most worth doing. That's why you should eliminate it from your vocabulary as soon as possible.

You can usually replace this phrase with the words—you guessed it—"I am" and "I have." And if you really want to add some punch, throw in the word "now." So instead of saying, "When I have enough time I will be a writer," say, "I am now a successful writer." Or "I now have a wonderful relationship with my children." Use your words to claim the right to do what you love now.

THE "NEVERS" OF PROSPERITY TALK

There are things you should never do or should do as seldom as possible. But if you catch yourself doing one of them, don't beat yourself up; simply counter the action with a positive affirmation and try to do better next time.

Never, ever waste your energy complaining that you have too many bills. Remember, what you talk about increases, and if you talk about having too many bills, they will only increase. Instead, affirm to yourself that you have fewer and fewer bills every day, and more and more money.

Never waste your time lamenting about how broke you are. Instead, use your words to express all the ways in which you can be fortunate.

Never talk about how hard it is going to be to do a certain thing you would like to do; this will just make it hard. Of course, there is no need to struggle or sacrifice. If you are open, the Universe will provide a way for you. Instead of using the word "hard," say to yourself, "I have now achieved my goal easily and effortlessly."

Never say you can't do something that you really want to do but feel you are not actually able to do it. Keep affirming to yourself, "I am now able to _____."

Never curse a person because they seem to have more money and success than you do. Holding jealousy and resentment will slow you down on your path to perfect prosperity. Replace your negative thoughts with loving ones.

WHAT YOU SAY COMES BACK TO YOU!

What you say about others comes back to you, so make it good! Some people may annoy you, others may anger you, but it is still to your benefit to focus on the good within them. By doing so, you clear the channel for prosperity. If you continually say bad things about others, focusing always on the negative, that is what you will get, both from yourself and from others.

You can increase your own prosperity by mentally and verbally affirming the prosperity of others. When you see a person who seems to be enjoying prosperity, mentally bless that person. Say to yourself, "I bless you and all your wonderful qualities." Don't waste your energy being jealous. Congratulate that person for their success. Send your love and prosperous thoughts out to them, knowing that this energy will return to you many times over. And remember: you are who you attract. If you are attracting wealthy, successful people into your life, you should be flattered and excited about where you are going!

CHAPTER 8

Prosperity Magic 101

I'd like to share with you another tool for manifesting prosperity, magic. Not the kind of magic magicians use—more like the kind of magic a fairy godmother uses. Magic means using certain tools to unleash the powers of your mind and of the Universe so that you can create a desired reality more effectively. The tools used in magic are willpower, intention, and a symbolic act. When you put the three together you have magic or, more specifically, a spell, which is a way for you to enact your desire or prayer. It is also the way that you bring your appeal to the Universe, showing it exactly what you wish to accomplish.

Let's cover the three components of a spell in more detail. Magic is always directed and powered by intention. You need to be specific about what you are trying to accomplish. When your intention is clear, your magic will work; when your intention is fuzzy and muddled, it is unlikely to work properly.

Let me give you an example of how a muddled intention can result in muddled magic. A friend asked me if I would work a money spell for her. We performed a general money spell together on the night of the next full moon. Shortly thereafter, her husband received a substantial raise and then she and her husband found a few hundred dollars hidden away in the attic. To top it off, someone offered to help pay her daughter's college expenses. All of this happened in a few short weeks. In my mind, there was no doubt that the money spell had worked, but when I talked to my friend, she seemed disappointed. Upon further prodding, she admitted that what she really wanted was to attract more clients for her business and become prosperous that way. Of course, the spell we worked was a general money spell, with the only stated intention being "to bring more money." Because we were not clear on our intentions, we were not really able to make the spell work the way my friend wanted it to.

It's best to clarify your true intention before you work prosperity magic. Ask yourself what is it you are trying to accomplish and what you really want. Try to state your intention in one simple idea such as "bring more clients," or "manifest more disposable income." Make sure that you state your intention clearly while working your prosperity spell. (This can be done by chanting, using an affirmation, or by repeating the sentence that encapsulates your desires.) If you keep your intention clear and follow the above steps, your prosperity magic is bound to be successful!

Although magic is powered by intention, it is always consummated with a symbolic act. No prosperity spell is complete without performing an act that somehow symbolizes your desire. The act can be as simple as raising your hands over your head to indicate increasing finances, or as elaborate as baking an entire meal of specially prepared "prosperity" food.

Keep in mind that nearly any symbolic act will do when working prosperity magic. Of course, the items used in a symbolic act should match your desire. For general prosperity spells, you can incorporate things like coins, dollars, honey, nuts, seeds, and shells. You can also use special prosperity colors, such as silver, gold, or green. (See the appendices for more ideas on things to include in a prosperity spell.)

For more specific spells, you'll want to match up your symbolic act with your unique desire. For instance, if you were working a spell to increase your chances of getting a job in the computer industry, you might want to use a picture of a computer, or you might stand near your home computer while you visualize yourself with your new job. If you are trying to land a book contract, you can include a book in your spell. If you are working on getting a raise, you might decide to draw out a pretend check and fill in your name along with the amount of the desired raise. To bring in more clients for your business, you could use a symbol of your business surrounded by little plastic people.

Of course, it's not the items you choose that are essential—even symbolic items aren't essential. It's what you do that really matters; after all, a symbolic act is an act! You will probably use gestures and symbols differently depending on what kind of change you are trying to create. For instance, if you're trying to get rid of something (say a debt or a poverty pattern), you may want to write the name of that something on a piece of toilet paper and flush it down the toilet. Or you can send a symbol of it sailing down the river in a tiny boat, ending up far, far away from you. You can also chant "be gone" while you move your hands back and forth away from your body.

If you are trying to bring something to you, you can draw a picture of it and sleep with it under your pillow for seven nights. Or you can psychically charge a specially prepared food with the energies of that something and then ingest the food. You can chant "come to me" while you move your hands back and forth toward your body.

Ultimately, only you can decide which symbolic act works best for your prosperity spell. Use my suggestions in this chapter as a starting point; then let your imagination take over!

In the end, the strength of a spell rests on your will power. (This is why we usually seal a spell by saying "This is my will, so must it be!")."Will power" means just what it says: the power to will something to happen. It also means exercising the right to make your own decisions and do what is right for you, even if others disagree.

Without will power, your spell will lack the psychic punch necessary to manifest your desire. With strong will power, your spell is likely to be a raging success! Magic works when you are truly "willing" for it to work.

Keep in mind that will power is not the same as desire. Anybody can have desire, and indeed, we all do. Will power is much more than this. To have will power is like saying, "Not only do I have a desire, but I will it to be true."

In order to will something to come true, you must believe that it is possible. Otherwise, it won't happen, whether we are talking about magic or ordinary life. Let me give you an example.

When I was twenty-one, I started my metaphysical career as a part-time astrologer. A year later, I quit my day job to pursue this path full-time. Many of my friends and family thought I was crazy. They didn't even recognize metaphysics as a valid career path. They kept asking me when I was going to get a job. They simply could not believe that it was possible for anyone to have a serious and successful career in metaphysics, but I knew it was possible. Not only did I know that it was possible, but I knew it was possible for me. I could see it in my mind as if it had already happened. I was "willing" it into being.

Today I am enjoying a successful career in metaphysics. Of course, I still have so much farther to go, but I wouldn't have even gotten this far if I hadn't first believed it was possible. Without that inner knowing, that belief that it could be real, I would still be waiting for my desire to manifest itself.

The same is true when you are working a prosperity spell. In order to be successful, you must know deep down that what you are asking for is possible and you must believe that it is possible for you. Then you must decide that you will have it. You must will it into existence.

If you find your will power wavering, it's best that you not do the spell right then. Take time to explore the source of this reaction. Ask yourself if it is coming from inside of you or outside of you. If you feel that it is coming from you, clarify your desire, then work the spell. If you feel it is coming from outside of you, practice some positive affirmations or do some cleansing before you do the spell. Either way, take the steps necessary to strengthen your will power; if your will power is strong, your magic is likely to be strong too!

Now that you more fully understand the components of a spell, it's time to get on to the meat of this chapter, the spells.

Below you'll find several simple recipes for prosperity magic. No prior experience is required. All that is necessary is an open mind and a loving heart.

PROSPERITY STONE DISH

Fill a bowl or a dish with green, gold, and earth colored stones. If you like, paint the outside of your dish green or gold, and embellish it with prosperity symbols such as a dollar sign, a treasure chest, or a four-leaf clover. Throw in a few coins.

Place both hands on the dish and say your prosperity affirmations over and over. Continue to chant until you feel that the stones and coins have been charged with prosperity energy. When you feel your chant reaching a peak, imagine green or gold light pouring into the top of your head and out the tips of your fingers. Envision your prosperity dish infused with this light. Take a moment to visualize yourself experiencing perfect prosperity. Slowly say your affirmations once again and give thanks. Rake your fingers through the stones every time you want some prosperity energy.

WALLET POWER

Put some tiny pieces of crystal or prosperity stones in your checkbook or wallet. Any green, gold, or earth-colored stone will do—citrine, tiger-eye, and green tourmaline work well.

Hold your wallet in your right hand and say to yourself, "By the powers of earth and stone, prosperity is mine!" Leave the stones in your wallet. Every time you open your wallet, repeat the above phrase.

A HOME RUN

Whenever you have a pressing debt or overdue bill, get a baseball or other fist-sized ball. Write the name and amount of your debt or bill on the ball. Take a minute to visualize the bill already paid and cleared up. Then grab the ball and throw it as far as you can or have someone throw it to you and hit it with a bat as hard as you can. Say to yourself, "Yes! I release this bill to the Universe, knowing that it is already taken care of! This is my will—so must it be!"

PROSPERITY POT

Plant a pot of basil, mint, or dill. As you bury the seeds, say to yourself, "As these seeds grow, so does my prosperity increase!" Write prosperity symbols and affirmations on the pot. Put the plant in a sunny place and watch your prosperity grow along with it.

POVERTY PATTERN FLUSH

If you have a debt or poverty pattern that is still bothering you, write it on a piece of toilet paper and flush it down the drain. Imagine yourself being freed from it. Practice this daily until it is gone from your life.

MONEY SHAKER

Mix together these dried ingredients in a clear glass or plastic jar: a pinch of ground allspice, cinnamon, cloves, dill, mint, and basil, a few ground almonds, a few dried black-eyed peas, a few coins, and maybe a dollar or two. Decorate the jar with prosperity symbols. Put a lid on the jar and keep it where you can see it often. Shake it any time you need a little extra money or to increase your prosperity.

PICTURE SPELL

Draw a picture symbolizing the money or other items you want to manifest. Be specific. Write these words on your picture: "By the powers of the Universal Source, the Ascended Masters, and the archangels, I now have _____ (your goal)." Chant this phrase while staring at a red candle, then put your picture in a safe place until your goal materializes.

PYRAMID CHARM

Write your desire at the bottom of a small piece of colored paper. (Any color will do, but you can pick a color from appendix C to match your desire.) Just above this, write it again, this time dropping the last letter of the phrase. For instance, if your desire is for a new car, write "new ca" above "new car." Continue writing your desire, each time moving up another line and dropping the last letter. Eventually, you will get to the point where you have formed a "pyramid" with your desire. Here is an example of what a pyramid charm would look like for a new car:

> *N*
> *NE*
> *NEW*
> *NEW C*
> *NEW CA*
> *NEW CAR*

When you are finished with the charm, sprinkle it with a little salt water and say,

> *I purify this charm*
> *Let it bring no harm!*
> *Bring me my wish*
> *And only this!*
> *This is my will—so it must be!*

Carry the completed charm in your pocket or wear it in your left shoe until your desire comes to you. When it does, burn the charm in a fireproof dish and give thanks to your higher power.

PROSPERITY INFUSION

Combine equal amounts of basil, mint, cinnamon, and clove (usually a teaspoon or less is plenty) into one cup of boiling water (more, if needed). Cover and let the mixture steep for 15-20 minutes. Strain this wonderful prosperity infusion and pour into your bathwater or soak a small towel in the infusion and wipe your entire body with it while showering. You can also use this infusion to wipe down floors, car seats, or anything that you want to charge with prosperity energy.

Feel free to substitute your favorite prosperity herbs in this recipe. (See appendix B for a list of prosperity herbs.) I sometimes add a little salt for purification and pepper for extra psychic "kick" to my prosperity infusions. You may want to do the same.

POCKET POWER

When you need to attract money quickly, get a little dried basil and some crushed maple leaves. Holding them in your right hand, say:

> *Basil and maple!*
> *Prosperity enable!*
> *Basil and maple*
> *Bring money to my table!*

Visualize yourself already having whatever it is that you need the money for and repeat this chant until the herbs are charged with your intent. When you can finally see this image clearly, say forcefully, "This is my will—so must it be!"

Carry the herbs in your pocket until the money comes to you. If you prefer, use a little pouch for your herbs to keep them from spilling out.

PROSPERITY CANDLE

On the night of a full moon, carve a dollar sign or other prosperity symbol on a large green candle. Light the candle, sit in front of it, and begin to breathe deeply. Start to imagine huge piles of money all around the candle. When you can see this in your mind, begin to chant softly,

> *Money, money*
> *Come to me!*
> *Let me see an increase!*

Continue chanting while you visualize huge piles of money moving closer to you. Move your hands back and forth to help direct the money. Open your arms wide and pull the money toward you. If you like, repeat this spell daily until you are satisfied with the increase in your income. This spell also works for getting a raise.

MANIFEST AN IDEAL JOB—FAST!

In red ink, write down all the qualities of your ideal job. Using a green marker, draw a circle around your list. This helps to connect the qualities and ensure that you attract a job that meets all of your criteria, rather than just some.

Next, get out your blow-dryer. (Yes, I am talking about that thing you dry your hair with.) Run the blow-dryer over your list while you say, "I now have my ideal job!" Say it eight, sixteen, or twenty-four times. Store the list in a red or green sock until your job comes to you.

MAKE PEACE WITH A BOSS OR CO-WORKER

There is no doubt that peace in the workplace is part of true prosperity. This spell is designed to help you create that. Find a hand mirror, preferably with a pink, blue, white, or green handle. (No red-handled mirrors for this one, please.) Use a blue eyeliner pencil or grease pen to write the name of the person you need to make peace with on the mirror. Write your name directly on top of theirs, so that the two names are merged together. Light a blue candle and sit quietly, looking into the mirror. Imagine a beam of sparkling blue or pink light shooting out of your heart onto the names on the mirror. Visualize the two of you getting along just fine. Repeat this spell at least three, five, or seven times and you will see a positive change in the relationship.

PROSPERITY BREAKFAST

Anoint a green candle with sandalwood oil. Prepare a bowl of oatmeal using whole-grain oats. Sweeten the cooked oats with pure maple syrup, and add some banana and ground cinnamon. While staring into the flame of your green candle, stir it all together clockwise. Visualize the oatmeal being infused with prosperity energy and prosperity symbols as you stir it. Eat your oatmeal by the light of the green candle, letting every bite fill you with prosperity.

PROSPERITY SOAP

Take a green bar of soap (Irish Spring® will work just fine). Using a nail or other sharp object, carve a symbol or words representing your desire directly onto the bar of soap. If you'd like, anoint it with a little sandalwood or jasmine oil. Light a few gold or green candles in your bathroom, turn off the lights, and get into the shower. Wash yourself all over with your prosperity soap and visualize your desire. To add extra punch, repeat this spell three days in a row.

TRAVELING PROSPERITY

To take prosperity energy with you wherever you go, get a small green or earth-colored pouch. Inside the pouch place some tiny sea shells, a little rice, one small clear quartz crystal, a few dark-colored stones, and a little dried mint. You can also write your major prosperity goals on a tiny piece of paper and slip it inside. Hang this pouch from your car rearview window, or carry it in your purse or suitcase when you travel.

SAFEKEEPING YOUR PROSPERITY

Some of us never achieve prosperity simply because we are afraid of losing it. Of course, no one can ever really take our prosperity from us. Nonetheless, the following spell can help you feel more secure that someone is watching over you and everything that is valuable to you.

Get three candles, one large and green, the other two red and orange and of any size. Using a nail or other sharp object, carve symbols and words to represent all that is valuable to you directly upon the green candle. Make sure you include things from the spiritual, emotional, mental, and physical planes. When you are finished, place the green candle between the red and the orange on a table and light them. Stare deeply into the green candle flame and say:

> I call upon the heavenly hosts
> to guard the things
> I love most!

Continue to build power as you repeat this chant over and over. You can play a drum while you chant, or slap your hands on your legs to create a rhythm. As the power builds, begin to imagine four spiritual beings coming forth, one from each of the four directions. See these beings clearly in your mind. You may see them as angels, saints, elementals, fairies, mythological animals, spiritual teachers, or any other positive being. Focus on attracting cooperative and loving beings who will be ready to keep all your valuables safe from harm. Continue to chant and drum until you can see your new prosperity guardians. For the strongest effect, repeat this spell several days in a row. Then know that your prosperity is safe.

CHAPTER 9

Prosperity Is Now!

YOU ALREADY HAVE ALL THAT YOU NEED— IT IS WITHIN YOU

You truly do not need to create prosperity—you only need to manifest the perfect prosperity that already exists within you. All of us have already manifested some physical world prosperity. Our bodies, the air we breathe, the food that we eat, the water we drink, the love in our hearts: these are all manifestations of our physical prosperity. By acknowledging that this prosperity is already in your life, you increase the amount that will come to you in the future.

No matter how unpleasant your life experience, there is always something to love in it. For instance, I once lived in a run-down, roach-infested house. No matter how much I scrubbed the shower, I could never really get it clean, and I had to be careful where I stepped in the bathroom because the floor was rotting away. Still, I had a beautiful pink rosebush by my window and a lovely mulberry tree in the backyard. I learned to love these things and I learned to love my house.

Eventually, I moved into a much nicer home. I believe that I was able to do this because I had stayed focused on appreciating the prosperity that I had already manifested in my life (such as my rose bush and mulberry tree), as little as it was. By doing so, I was able to manifest a much greater prosperity. Now, every time I move, it is to nicer and nicer homes.

The same principle can work for you. The rest of this chapter is dedicated to exploring the three keys to honoring your prosperity in the now: gratitude, responsibility, and awareness. By learning to honor the prosperity that already exists in your life, you can open yourself up to higher and higher levels of riches and fulfillment.

GRATITUDE

Gratitude is the stuff prosperity is made of. Wherever there is gratitude, there can be no fear or worry. And where there is no fear or worry, prosperity will come. When you are filled with gratitude, you become an open channel for prosperity energy. You can't help but be prosperous!

Never underestimate the power of a grateful heart when it comes to manifesting prosperity. It can turn even the worst situation into something pleasant and prosperous. I have known many people who have been through horrible, traumatic situations but have gone on to be extremely successful. What these people all had in common was one thing: gratitude. No matter how little they had, they were always grateful. Even after they moved into better situations, they were still grateful for the lessons they learned from their previous experiences.

On the other hand, I have known scores of people who have been given much in their lives, but aren't grateful for an ounce of it. These people appear prosperous, but inside, they are miserable, emotionally and spiritually impoverished. That's because it's impossible to experience true prosperity without gratitude. Even the best of circumstances seem unbearable if you don't have a grateful heart. Without one, you can't feel the joy radiating in your own life. All you have is a relentless desire to have more.

No matter how much or how little you have been given in life, you have to be grateful if you want more. It does absolutely no good to sit around moaning and groaning about how you don't have this or you don't have that. Sure, I bet there are some things that you would like to have. But if you choose to stay focused on how little you have, rather than on being grateful, you will continue to have less and less each day. If you are really interested in increasing your prosperity, you will first have to work on gratitude. Then you will find your prosperity increasing easily and naturally.

One of the best ways to increase your prosperity is to create a gratitude list. This is a simple exercise, one that anyone can do. At the top of a page, write "Things I Am Grateful For," and list them. Include as many things as possible, and don't limit your list only to material things. Anything that inspires your gratitude can go on your list—nothing is too large or too small. Some of the things on my list are chocolate, a happy marriage, psychic abilities, comfortable shoes, and my beautiful son. Keep your list in a convenient place, and try to read it every day. Feel free to change it as time goes on.

If you want to be really creative, you can also try making a collage of your list. Start by getting out a sheet of your favorite colored paper (see appendix C for more information on colors). Draw pictures and symbols to represent the things you are most grateful for. Hang your gratitude picture in a place where you can see it often. Whenever something new and wonderful comes into your life, add it to your picture.

You may also find it useful to start a daily gratitude journal. I was lucky enough to find a specially designed gratitude journal at a local scrapbook store. It has the word "gratitude" written in gold on the front. On the inside, each page has a different gratitude-related quote printed at the top with a place to add my own gratitude thoughts. Of course, you don't have to purchase a special notebook to create a gratitude journal; any notebook will do. Find one that is attractive to you, write "gratitude" on the front cover, and use the pages to record your daily (or occasional) thoughts of gratitude. If you like, you can also use it to record some of your favorite uplifting quotes or affirmations.

If you want to be truly prosperous, practice giving thanks several times a day. Give thanks when you get paid. Give thanks when you come home at night and when you go to sleep at night. Give thanks when you eat.

If you think you don't have anything to give thanks for, I encourage you to think again. If you are reading this book, you have at least one thing to be grateful for: the ability to read and write. There are literally millions of people in the world who can't read or write, and you are fortunate enough to be able to read this book!

Consider your health. If you are lucky enough to be healthy, take a moment to give thanks. If not, you can still be grateful to have use of your senses and your arms and legs. There is always someone in the world worse off than you.

Give thanks every day for each person in your life and the lessons they teach you. Is there someone in your life driving you nuts? Don't waste your time complaining about that person—it will only give them more cause to keep annoying you. Instead, be grateful for what you are learning from that person.

Maybe you don't feel like giving thanks because you've lost someone important to you. You can still be grateful for the time you had with them, for all the love, beauty, and lessons that you shared together.

Practice giving thanks for your material possessions, no matter how little they may seem. Do you have running water, electricity, or a functioning refrigerator? No matter what you find to be grateful for, give thanks! You will find your prosperity increasing on all levels!

"Gratitude talk" is a way of talking that inspires gratitude and thanks. It is a little bit different from simply giving thanks and it can be used on a regular basis during conversations. All you need to practice gratitude talk is an open mind and a few basic phrases such as these:

- I'm really glad that…
- Isn't it great that…
- I'm grateful that…
- Thank God/dess…
- I appreciate…
- It's wonderful that…
- How marvelous that…

Use these phrases often in your conversations and you will be practicing gratitude talk. Gratitude talk can also take the form of affirmations. Use any of the phrases to create personalized gratitude affirmations.

One of the best ways to express your gratitude (and increase your prosperity) is to say a daily gratitude prayer. You can be spontaneous and improvise a new prayer every day. If you have difficulty doing this, you may want to write an "official" gratitude prayer and repeat it every day. This method works well because it keeps things simple and focuses your gratitude. If you don't feel like writing your own gratitude prayer, try this one that my husband uses daily. I challenge you to say this every day for three months and see what happens.

The Gratitude Prayer
by Brian Hinkle

I thank you God/Goddess
I thank you Jesus
I thank the Higher Power
I thank the Ascended Masters
I thank you Saint Francis
I thank you Saint Germaine
I thank all those who guide me through my lives
And I send my loving gratitude
To each and every living creature
—Amen

RESPONSIBILITY

Prosperity and responsibility go hand and hand. You cannot have one without the other. With each new level of prosperity comes an increased amount of responsibility because you have more to be responsible for. There is a nice flip side to this: the more responsible you are, the easier it will be for you to become prosperous. Responsibility is a form of enacted gratitude. Being responsible shows the Universe that you fully appreciate what you have been given, not only in mind and heart, but in deed as well. On the other hand, being irresponsible with either your material or non-material goods shows the Universe that you don't really appreciate what has been given to you, regardless of what you may say.

Responsibility is also an important part of ensuring future increases in your prosperity. Dealing with your existing prosperity responsibly gives the Universe the green light to send you more, whereas treating your existing prosperity irresponsibly shows that you can't handle the prosperity that you have, let alone more.

There is an old saying that God never gives you more than you can handle. I believe this is true whether we are talking about hardships or prosperity. If you haven't learned to properly manage your existing prosperity, more prosperity would only complicate your life. This is one of the reasons why we see some people who win the lottery ending up bankrupt or worse off than when they started.

Many of us never aspire to the highest levels of prosperity because deep down inside, we don't want the extra responsibility. It's okay if you feel that way. You can choose how prosperous you are willing to become, and consequently how much you will be responsible for. But if you want to reach the highest levels of prosperity, you will have to be willing to accept the additional responsibilities.

For instance, let's say your salary suddenly tripled. Obviously, such a significant increase would open up many new avenues of self-fulfillment. However, it would also require that you adjust to a new level of financial responsibility. For starters, you would need to make a new budget. Depending on your original salary, you may need to hire someone to help you create this new budget. You may also want to invest some of your money. This would require that you spend time learning about the various types of investments. At the very least, you would want to consult with someone who has expertise in investments. Either way, it would take some effort to figure out how to best invest your money.

There would be many other issues to deal with in this situation. For instance, you would have to ask yourself how it would affect your taxes. You would need to decide how much of your new money you would like to share with others. How much should you save? How much should go toward paying off bills? How much should you allow yourself to spend?

Of course, additional responsibilities aren't limited to increases in physical prosperity alone. No matter how your prosperity increases, you will have to make adjustments. If you suddenly find yourself more prosperous on the emotional level, you will have to adjust to the new quality or quantity of relationships in your life. If you find yourself feeling prosperous on a spiritual level, you will have to learn how to manage your new spiritual abilities. If you have just moved up a level in the area of mental prosperity, you will have to deal with the additional responsibility that comes with an advanced intellect. Regardless of the area, each new level of prosperity brings increased responsibility.

As you can see, responsibility is a major part of being prosperous. But don't let this rain on your prosperity parade. Even if you have never been responsible in the past, you can start today. All you really need is a little bit of effort and an understanding of "proper use" and "proper care."

You are responsible for using what you have properly, no matter how little or how much it may be. You must use what you have in a way that is beneficial and uplifting to yourself and others. For instance, using your car to drive back and forth to a job that you love is a proper use of a car, but using your car to endanger another person's life is an improper (not to mention profane) use of an automobile.

Money can also be used properly or improperly. Spending your money on the things that bring you joy is using it properly. Purchasing something just because you were pressured into buying it is an improper use of money.

Even something that is seemingly insignificant can have proper and improper uses. Take cosmetics, for example. If you are putting on makeup simply because you want to accentuate your naturally beautiful features, then in my opinion, you understand the proper use of makeup. If you are putting on makeup to deceive somebody about how you really look, or because you are disgusted with your true self, then you are using it improperly.

Your responsibility also extends to non-physical, intangible forms of prosperity. Some intangible manifestations of prosperity are your mind, your heart, and your time. To reach your highest prosperity, you will want to make sure that you use these intangibles properly. Using your mind to think positive thoughts about yourself and others would constitute a proper use; using your mind to focus on the negative constantly would be an improper use of your mental abilities.

Your time is another very important intangible resource. A proper use of your time would be anything that allows you to celebrate, smile, or feel good. An improper use of your time would be brooding or throwing a prolonged self-pity party.

Ultimately, only you can decide what are proper or improper uses of your resources. I encourage you to start thinking about this matter today. By using what you already have properly, you will open yourself up to higher and higher levels of prosperity.

In addition to using what you have properly, you are also responsible for taking good care of what you have, regardless of how much or how little it is. The way you treat your existing prosperity is how you show the Universe whether or not you are ready to receive more. Again, this applies whether we are talking about tangible or intangible forms of prosperity. Let's take money, for example. The way you treat your current amount of money demonstrates whether or not you are ready to receive more. That's why you should never wrinkle or wad your money up into a disorganized pile. If you do, you are showing disrespect for money, and your attitude certainly will not bring in as much money as if you had treated it respectfully. Treat your money with love, and keep it neat and organized. Then you're sure to bring in more.

The same thing is true when dealing with all material assets, including bank accounts, cars, homes, and clothing. Never treat your material possessions with disregard or disrespect, unless of course you are not interested in experiencing material prosperity. Treat all your possessions the way you would treat a beloved friend and you will find your prosperity increasing on all levels.

You also need to take good care of your non-material forms of prosperity. Take, for example, your heart. One of the best ways to increase your prosperity is to open your heart to somebody who cares about you. One of the fastest ways to reduce your prosperity is to squander your love on someone who obviously isn't going to return it in kind. Consider also your body. No matter how little material wealth you have, you must still have a body if you are reading this. Unfortunately, many people look at having a body as a liability. This is why so many people are obsessed with getting to heaven or ascending.

In reality, a body is an outer manifestation of inner prosperity, a wonderful vehicle for experiencing life on the physical plane. As such, it should be treated with respect and care. Feed it foods that nurture it, keep it in good shape, and share it only with other people who honor it. Then you will be showing the Universe that you are ready for perfect prosperity.

Whether your concern is material or non-material prosperity, you must treat what you already have with great care if you are to manifest more. Everything in your life is no less than an expression of the Divine Source made manifest in physical form. Treat it as such.

If you don't have as much prosperity as you'd like, you might want to ask yourself if there are any ways that you could be more responsible with what you have already been given. Take the time to look at every area of your life. Start with your finances. Is there a way you could be more responsible with money? Maybe you need to make a budget, or perhaps you need to open up a different bank account. Maybe you simply need to treat your money with more respect; maybe you need to make sure you set aside a little for enjoyment.

Move on to your material possessions. How do you treat your home? Do you keep it clean and uncluttered, or do you let every room overflow with stuff? Perhaps a little house-cleaning would show the Universe that you are really serious about having prosperity.

Look at how you treat your jewelry, your clothing, your car—any material possession you have. What kind of messages are you sending out to the Universe by the way you treat these things? Maybe it is time to send a different message, especially if you haven't reached the level of prosperity that you'd like.

Move on to your non-material things. Start with your opportunities. Ask yourself if you have really tried to take advantage of the opportunities around you. If the answer is no, it may be time to start taking advantage of your existing opportunities instead of asking for more.

Look at your relationships. Have you really been responsible here? Or have you taken some relationships for granted? Perhaps it is time to do something to show the people in your life how much you love them.

Move on to any other area of importance to you—your mind, your body, your creativity, and your time, for instance. Examine your life carefully. Leave no stone unturned. If it causes you discomfort or guilt to think about a certain area, I encourage you to move into it even more deeply. The things that cause you the most discomfort are often the things you stand to gain the most from.

I am not saying that if you are experiencing financial frustration, it automatically means you have been irresponsible. There are many reasons that people experience financial frustration, not the least of which may be society's attitude toward them. Nonetheless, if you want to increase your capacity for prosperity, you must first increase your capacity for responsibility.

AWARENESS

Congratulations! You've almost made it to the end of the book. Before we say goodbye, I'd like to share with you the final key to honoring prosperity in the now: awareness. Your ability to experience and acknowledge prosperity ultimately rests on one thing—your awareness. Without awareness, there can be no gratitude or responsibility. Indeed, without awareness, you will have no sense of what to be grateful or responsible for. Thus, awareness is a prerequisite for experiencing true prosperity.

"Awareness" means being fully conscious and knowledgeable about yourself and your patterns. This is important to prosperity work because your patterns have created the prosperity you are currently experiencing. Without awareness, you won't know which patterns are creating what or how to go about changing these patterns. With awareness, you are more readily equipped to make positive change.

Awareness also allows you to be conscious of the prosperity that already exists in your life. It can make you feel like the richest, most prosperous person in the world, where a low level of awareness can make you feel like the poorest, most miserable person on earth. Without awareness, you will never actually feel prosperous, regardless of how much money or good fortune you have. That's because physical circumstances don't determine true prosperity; awareness does. The more awareness you have, the more prosperous you will feel on all levels.

Of course, to be aware, you have to be willing to pay attention. You can't just sleepwalk your way through prosperity work. If you want to experience true prosperity, you have to be here, now, or you will continue to be a victim of your own poverty patterns. If you pay attention long enough, sooner or later you will see something you don't like. This is part of being human and part of becoming aware. You don't have to let this intimidate you. When you become aware of something you aren't comfortable with, ultimately it is so you can turn it into something you are comfortable with. Otherwise that nasty little thing just keeps lurking around in the dark corners of your life.

Although being aware may seem like hard work, it is just as difficult (if not more so) to choose to remain unaware. It takes a great deal of energy to continue to push the truth of your life under the surface. Furthermore, unaware individuals are rarely conscious of the prosperity in their lives, regardless of how truly privileged they may be.

The path of awareness is the path of clarity and truth. People who choose to remain unaware are always looking for someone else to show them the way to happiness or prosperity. Highly aware people usually do not need to be told what to do—they already know. Which of these would you prefer to be?

Awareness is also about deliberate action. "Deliberate action" means carefully considering the effects of each and every potential move and then acting accordingly. To be truly prosperous, you must transform your poverty patterns into prosperity habits. It is impossible to do this without deliberate action.

Deliberate action means acting with a purpose. Naturally, when you're focused on prosperity work, that purpose will be to increase your prosperity. Of course, all action (deliberate or otherwise) has a purpose, but most of the time we are not aware of the purpose. How many of us realize that every self-critical comment we make only serves to keep us from true prosperity? With deliberate action, you not only have a purpose but you are also aware of your purpose.

Deliberate action is intentional action—it is charged with your intentions. It's one thing to automatically fold your money up neatly in your wallet because that's the way you were always taught to do it. It is another thing to do this consciously with the intention that it will increase your prosperity.

Some people resist the idea of deliberate action because they don't believe they have any control over their own actions. You will often hear these people say, "But I can't help it!"

My reply to that is, "Yes, you can! In fact, you are the only one who can help it." By acting with a purpose and considering the effects of each of your actions, you can begin to create a more prosperous life for yourself. The following exercises can help you get started.

Do this exercise the next time you have to make an important decision, especially one that directly involves your prosperity. Take some time to be alone in a quiet and relaxed setting. Turn off the TV and the phone, shut the door, and plan on working on nothing else except this decision for a while.

The first key to acting with awareness is to figure out exactly what you are trying to decide. Get out a sheet of paper and write a short one- or two-sentence description of the matter in question. If you like, use a sheet of appropriately colored paper to symbolize the issue at hand.

Next, figure out what your feelings are about this decision. Perhaps the best way is to write them down. If you find it difficult to write for long periods of time, use a tape recorder. Either way, do not stop until you have recorded all your feelings about this decision.

Next make a list of your possible choices in this matter. Write down whatever comes to mind. Do not edit your choices; this is just the brainstorming phase. Remember the time to make a decision isn't now. Finally, ask yourself which one of these choices feels right to you. Notice that I did not ask which choice seems most logical or which one seems easiest to carry out. You are looking for the choice that feels right, the one that would best advance the prosperity of everyone involved. If there is any confusion or question about which choice is best, look at your motivations. The choice that is motivated by a sincere desire to help everyone involved (including yourself) is almost always the right one.

Practice this exercise for all your major decisions. After a little while, you will be able to do this entire process mentally for any decision in a matter of a few minutes.

PROSPERITY AWARENESS MEDITATION

Find some quiet time alone. Sit comfortably on the floor or in your favorite chair. Begin to breathe deeply. Close your eyes. Focus on you breath for one to five minutes. After your breathing has become deeply relaxed, begin to shift your mind to the issue of prosperity. Start to think consciously of all the ways prosperity energy has expressed itself in your life. Focus on this for a few minutes, allowing concrete examples to come to mind. If you find yourself drifting to other thoughts, gently redirect your mind back to the issue at hand. Next begin to focus on all the ways you would like to see prosperity energy manifested in your life. Imagine prosperity energy flowing through you to manifest these things. Try to pay attention to how this feels. If it seems difficult for the energy to flow through you, ask your guides or your Higher Power why this is so. Pay attention to any images, feelings, or sensations you receive in response to this question. Finally, ask yourself (and your Higher Power) if there is anything you need to know regarding your prosperity issues. Again, pay attention to anything received after posing this question. Then close your meditation with a prayer of thanks and gratitude.

Some of the messages you receive during this exercise may startle you with their stark honesty. Truthfully, awareness is not for the faint of heart, but then again, neither is the pursuit of prosperity. Give yourself a hug for having the courage to try.

Afterword

Prosperity is a journey. We all start at different places and ultimately we all arrive at different destinations. You can't judge your progress by comparing yourself to others. Prosperity is not about where you are; it's about how far you've come. Each new level of success is important, no matter how small it may seem at the time.

When things are going well, you may be tempted to stop doing your prosperity work. Please don't. To continue to grow takes sustained attention on your part. A prosperity consciousness takes time to develop, and above all, it takes effort to maintain. It's not something that you do only once and then it's over.

The human potential to manifest prosperity is limitless and always evolving. The amount of prosperity you manifest today is a tiny fraction of what you could manifest in just a few years with a little daily prosperity work. Eventually, the benefits of your prosperity consciousness will radiate outward into every area of your life and every person you come into contact with.

I hope you have enjoyed reading this book as much as I enjoyed writing it. May you experience perfect prosperity!

Appendix

Inside this appendix, you'll find listings for all kinds of wonderful things you can use to increase your prosperity. Feel free to substitute any of these into the prosperity spells and exercises I have given you. Or, if you like, be creative and use them to invent your own prosperity increasing exercises.

As always, the only limit is your own imagination.

Prosperity Stones and Metals

Stones, like people, have their own energies. The following is a list of those stones that can help manifest prosperity. Keep in mind that any gold, green, or earth-colored stone can be somewhat helpful in manifesting prosperity.

- Adamite
- Amethyst
- Atelestite
- Bertrandite
- Bixbyite
- Bolivarite
- Childrenite
- Citrine
- Clear quartz
- Concretion
- Copper
- Domeykite
- Dundasite
- Flint
- Fossils
- Gold
- Green quartz
- Green and yellow tourmaline
- Heinrichite
- Hematite
- Jade
- Jasper (especially picture jasper)

- Jet
- Kernite
- Kyanite
- Lead
- Lodestone
- Messelite
- Obsidian
- Onyx
- Pyrite
- Rickardite
- Ruby
- Sapphire
- Selenite
- Silver
- Smokey quartz
- Tiger-eye
- Tin
- Topaz
- White opal

WHAT YOU CAN DO WITH PROSPERITY STONES

- Wear them in your socks.
- Place them in the bath (just make sure you take them out before you pull the plug).
- Make an elixir by soaking your stone in a bowl of water for twenty-four hours in the sun or in the moonlight. Drink it the next day for a prosperity supercharge. You can also charge juice or wine the same way, just make sure you use stones that are completely non-toxic for this method. Put the elixir in a spray bottle and use to spray your money, wallet, home, and work.
- Wear the stone(s) in a pouch or as jewelry.

- Place the stone(s) near the front door of your home or office.
- Hang the stone(s) with a green, gold, or silver ribbon from the rearview mirror in your car.
- Place the stone(s) on your desk or near your workspace.
- Decorate your coffee table with them.
- Wear tiny pieces in your bra.
- Place them on your home altar.
- Place them under or in your pillow.
- Keep them in your piggy bank.
- Make a rock garden, inside or outside your house.
- Carry them in your wallet or purse.
- Put large stones at the four corners of your home.

There are many more things you can do with prosperity stones and metals. To learn more about magical stones, see *Love Is in the Earth* by Melody or the chapter on crystals and gems in *Folkways* by Patricia Telesco. Above all, let your heart and your imagination guide you.

PROSPERITY HERBS AND FOOD

Plants, like stones, have their own unique vibrations. Many plants are thought to be helpful in attracting money, success, and prosperity. For your convenience, I have included a short list of these.

- Allspice
- Almond
- Banana
- Basil
- Beans (of all kinds)
- Blackberry
- Brazil nuts
- Buckwheat
- Cashew
- Carob
- Cedar
- Chamomile
- Chocolate (my personal favorite!)
- Cinnamon
- Clove
- Dill
- Fern
- Fig
- Flax
- Ginger
- Goldenseal
- Grapes
- Honeysuckle

- Jasmine
- Lettuce (and all salad greens)
- Macadamia nuts
- Maple (leaves, wood, and syrup)
- Marjoram
- Mint
- Nutmeg
- Oak
- Oats
- Onion
- Orange
- Parsley
- Patchouli
- Pear
- Peanuts and peanut butter
- Peas
- Pecans
- Pine
- Pineapple
- Poppy seeds
- Rice
- Sandalwood
- Sesame seeds
- Tea
- Tomato
- Vervain
- Wheat

Things You Can Do with Prosperity Herbs

- Sprinkle the powdered herb around the inside and outside of your home or work.
- Hang herb sprigs from the rearview mirror in your car.
- Decorate your kitchen with dried herb sprigs or potted plants.
- Carry them in your pocket.
- Combine two or three prosperity herbs and wear them in a pouch.
- Use them in your potpourri pot.
- Wear an oil made from your favorite herb.
- Write your affirmations on the outside of a pot with a permanent marker and grow your favorite herbs.
- Brew a tea.
- Create infusions for washing down floors or using in the bath.
- Anoint wallets, checkbooks, money, and any other important item with their oils.
- Season salads and sauces with them.

Things You Can Do with Prosperity Foods

- Make meals out of them.
- Grow them in your garden.
- Place them on your windowsill.
- Fill your fruit bowl with them (grapes, bananas, oranges).
- Write your desire on a piece of paper and bury it in the ground with a prosperity food.
- Consume the food at the end of prosperity spells in order to ground yourself.
- Snack on them.
- Create a prosperity rattle by filling an old peanut butter jar with beans, nuts, or seeds.
- Give them as gifts to help spread the prosperity around.
- When appropriate, decorate your altar with them.
- Leave them as offerings to ensure that a prosperity spell works.

There are many more things you can do with prosperity foods and herbs. To learn more about the magical uses of plants, see Scott Cunningham's *Encyclopedia of Magical Herbs*. Use your imagination to find uses for the foods that are most helpful.

COLOR

Color has a profound effect on all levels. On a psychological level, certain colors seem to make us feel happy (bright hues) while others tend to make us feel depressed (dreary and washed-out colors). Colors even seem to have physical effects—some colors can make us feel warm (the brighter, more red or orange ones), where others seem to make us feel cool (darker, more bluish or green colors).

Color also has a great effect on the psychic level. Each color is a different vibration of Universal Energy. Each vibration (color) can be used to manifest a specific energy into the physical world from the psychic plane.

Traditionally, certain colors (such as brown, green, and gold) were thought to be helpful in attracting prosperity. The other colors were thought to "rule" other areas of life and were not generally considered part of prosperity work. However, I believe that every color has at least some application in manifesting true prosperity. Below you will find some suggestions for using color in your prosperity work, along with an alphabetized list of colors and their effects on prosperity.

WAYS TO USE COLOR
TO MANIFEST PROSPERITY

- Wear it as clothing and jewelry.
- Eat it—consume a food or drink of that color.
- Write or draw with it.
- Decorate with it.
- Paint with it.
- Use it in your prosperity spells.
- Use it in the form of colored paper for your prosperity work.
- Collect it in the form of flowers, seeds, shells, and other natural things that are of the same color.
- Burn a candle of the appropriate color.
- Cover your home altar in a colored cloth.
- Visualize yourself surrounded in a bubble of your favorite prosperity colors.

COLORS

Black—A little goes a long way. Traditionally, black is used for protection and banishment. For prosperity work, use black to break up old ways of doing things and create *major* change. Black is great for banishing poverty patterns and debts. It is also useful when you need to get past a financial plateau. It helps dissolve resistance and stagnation.

Blue—The color of peace, protection, wisdom, and spirituality. Use blue (especially light blue) when writing your prosperity story or clarifying your prosperity goals. Also use blue to stimulate harmony and agreement in financial matters. Royal blue is the best color to use in seeking angelic or divine assistance in manifesting prosperity.

Brown—A wonderful prosperity color! Wear it often to attract money or material comforts into your life. It is also associated with home and family. Use it to get your house in order, manifest a new home, or increase the amount of material possessions within your home. Brown, the color of wood, is an excellent grounding color. If you have trouble organizing your finances or keeping a job, brown may be the perfect color for you.

Burgundy—Use burgundy to stimulate inspiration in business dealings. You can also use it to attract money or material comforts. It is excellent for stimulating grounded energy and long-term change. Burgundy helps direct courage and will power into practical and profitable ventures. It may work slightly more slowly (but longer) than other forms of red.

Gold—Traditionally, gold rules prosperity, good luck, money, and fortune. It is also associated with vitality and health. Use gold for prosperity work of all kinds, especially when your purpose is to increase your income. It is also useful whenever you are in a financial bind. Use gold to ensure that your prosperity goals will bring you happiness. Gold also works to give you the upper hand in gambling or in any kind of competition. Gold is useful for replacing the vitality that is sometimes destroyed by too much work. Use it to seek the favor of influential men.

Gray—Gray rules balance, discernment, and maturity—the wise woman or man inside of you. Gray is useful for adding depth and seriousness to your prosperity work. It is also helpful for unlocking the knowledge about yourself that is necessary to truly manifest prosperity. Use it to create a balance between physical and non-physical forms of prosperity. Gray is a combination of the energies of white and black.

Green—Green is a traditional prosperity color. It is associated with good fortune, growth, wealth, fertility, new beginnings, and health. Use it for prosperity work involving a desired increase. Avoid using it when the goal is a desired decrease, such as if ridding yourself of a debt or poverty pattern. In America, green is the color of money. Use green to draw more money into your life.

Lavender—Lavender is a blend of purple and white. It is associated with good works, spiritual protection, success, and blessings. Use it to increase the financial value of any charity or spiritually based endeavor. It is also useful for attracting benevolent spiritual beings to assist in prosperity work. Wear lavender to attune your prosperity goals with the spiritual. Lavender is a much more gentle vibration of purple and can be used by those who find the energies of purple too intense.

Magenta—Magenta is a deep red with some purple in it. Use it to make your prosperity work proceed quickly. Wear it to ensure success in matters of the highest importance. Magenta combines the two most intense colors, purple and red, and should be used with respect and moderation. Magenta tends to work faster than most reds, although burgundy may be better for more long-term projects.

Orange—Orange is traditionally associated with abundance and prosperity. It also rules good luck, friendship, enthusiasm, success, and creativity. In short, it is one of the best prosperity colors. Orange works quickly, because it is a warm color as opposed to a cool color. Use orange only when you are truly ready for change to happen suddenly. Orange helps to attract friendships and opportunities that would be useful to advance your prosperity and is the perfect networking color. Also, use it to attract benevolence of all kinds or to reverse bad luck. When you need a little bit of get-up-and-go, wear some orange. To maintain your enthusiasm over a long period of time, use orange with green or gold. In general, use orange to attract pleasant and prosperous situations.

Peach—Peach combines the energies of orange and white. It represents the purest, untainted forms of prosperity. Use it to keep your mind focused on prosperity and to manifest your highest ideals. Peach attracts good luck and synchronicity of the greatest kind. It is also useful for forging deep friendships with benevolent spiritual beings, such as angels or saints.

Pink—Pink is associated with love, friendship, emotional healing, and security. Pink helps heal poverty patterns and gives the confidence needed to aspire to the next level of prosperity. Use pink in all prosperity issues involving close friends or family, for instance when you are trying to manifest enough money to send your children to college. Also wear pink in times of great financial transition to help you feel safe. There is no better color for emotional prosperity than pink.

Purple—Purple is associated with success of all kinds, psychic powers, spirituality, and protection. Use purple to reverse bad financial luck or to appeal to the spirit world to bring you financial fortune. Also use it to ensure success of all kinds. It can be helpful when you use psychic powers to advance your prosperity work. Purple is a very intense color. It combines the energies of red and blue, and it vibrates neither quickly nor slowly but outside of temporal time. Use it with care. If you are in a bind that you need to clear up quickly, use purple with orange. Also use this combination to gain the favor of influential people.

Red—Red rules energy, strength, courage, and will power. It is also traditionally associated with inspiration, sexual desire, and romantic love. Use it whenever you need courage or will power to carry out your dreams, or when you need to draw in extra inspiration. Red is also useful for stimulating energy and motivation. Red, like orange, tends to create dramatic change quickly. Use it with moderation. When using it for long periods of time, balance it out with blue or green. Wear red for protection when you think your prosperity is being threatened by an outside source.

Silver—Silver is another traditional prosperity color, sacred to the Moon Goddess. It rules divine protection and access to the Higher Power. Use it in prosperity work to clear out obstacles and repeal stagnant or negative energies. You can also use it to petition angels and spiritual beings on your behalf. Silver can also be used to seek the favor of influential women. Being one of the metallic colors, silver is considered especially magical.

Turquoise—Use turquoise to stimulate clarity or agreement concerning prosperity and financial matters. Also use it to attract angelic assistance in manifesting wealth and money. Turquoise is a calming color and is appropriate for prosperity work that requires great patience. This color is a blend of blue and green. It can embody your prosperity work with the most powerful forms of spirituality and healing. Use it with gold or silver to win success in business.

White—White is associated with protection, purity, and wholeness. It is also considered sacred to the Goddess. Use white when contacting spirit helpers for assistance in prosperity work, or when trying to manifest your highest dreams. Use it whenever you feel your prosperity being threatened by destructive forces. White is a safe color to use for nearly any prosperity work. All pastels and lighter shades combine the energies of their base color plus white.

Yellow—Yellow rules creativity, imagination, communication, commerce, and the intellect. It is also linked to inspiration and knowledge. Use it for all prosperity work involving creative endeavors. It can positively influence the signing of contracts or the negotiation of payment. It is useful for all affairs involving employment or banking and for education or funding for education. When your prosperity depends on persuading another to your viewpoint, use yellow.

POWER ANIMALS

Power animals—sometimes called totems—are actually human archetypes in animal form. According to Native Americans and some other indigenous people, the spirit of every animal has its unique energy and special abilities, along with its own strengths and weaknesses. For instance, the wolf is beneficial for learning to work among groups, but the spirit of the heron teaches one to be self-reliant. There is a power animal for nearly everything under the sun, from healing to creativity to being a strong warrior. This section covers those totems I have found to be most relevant to prosperity work.

Power animals are accessed in many of the same ways that other benevolent spiritual beings, such as angels, are through prayer, meditation, magic, and visualization. Many modern Shamans undertake a shamanic journey to locate a power animal. However, I have found you do not need to be familiar with advanced shamanic techniques in order to work with a power animal. Many times, power animals will come to you spontaneously or as a result of your seeking them out. Naturally, some animals are of more assistance in helping you manifest prosperity than others. Below you'll find some suggestions for working with powers animals, along with an alphabetized list of the ones I consider to be some of the most effective for prosperity.

WAYS TO INVOKE THE ENERGIES OF A POWER ANIMAL

- Place a small statue of the animal in your home or altar.
- Observe the animal in the wild.
- Decorate your house with colorful posters, photographs, or drawings of the animal.
- Keep a stuffed-animal version in your office, car, or bedroom. Beanie babies are great for this.
- Get your stationery and checks printed with the image of the animal.
- Change the screen saver on your computer to an image of the animal.
- Do a shamanic journey or guided meditation to meet your animal.
- Read as much as you can about your power animal.
- Do a special ceremony or set up an altar to honor the animal.

- Write a poem about the animal.
- Make up a dance imitating the animal's movements and activities.
- Buy and read some children's books about your animal.
- Try to learn to imitate the sound of your animal.
- Above all, simply ask for its assistance.

PROSPERITY POWER ANIMALS

Ant—The ant gives you the stamina, fortitude, and endurance necessary to make dreams a reality. The ant brings success and prosperity, but only if you are willing to put in the work. The ant also teaches us how to work with others so that we can build something bigger than we can build alone. Call upon the ant for any matter concerning work, or for long-term development of dreams.

Bat—A symbol of transformation, the bat helps to instigate new life patterns and to find the way through the darkness. Call upon the bat in times of financial crisis. The bat will assist you in letting go of old patterns that stand in the way of new prosperity.

Bear—The bear helps to find the inner and outer resources necessary for survival. One of the bear's favorite foods is honey; the bear can lead you to the sweetness and joy of life.

It also assists with uncovering hidden skills and abilities to further your movement toward prosperity. Call upon the bear to help make all your dreams come true.

Beaver—The beaver is a very hard worker who can help increase your prosperity by inspiring persistence, creativity, and inventiveness in work issues. The beaver is the master builder of the animal kingdom and can be called upon to build a solid foundation for all your dreams.

Bee—The busy bee helps with all matters concerning work and productivity, and is considered by many to bring good luck. Like the bear, the bee is associated with honey and all the richness and sweetness that this implies. It is also one of nature's most prolific pollinators. Call upon the bee to pollinate any creative projects you may have or to help you accomplish the impossible.

Bison/Buffalo—Associated with prosperity and abundance by the North American Plains Indians, the buffalo can help sustain you on the physical and spiritual levels. Call upon the buffalo for all your prosperity needs.

Bull/Cow—Associated with the astrological sign of Taurus, the bull can be helpful in manifesting money, possessions, and wealth. You can also call upon the bull to aid in creativity and productivity. One word of caution: If the bull appears in your life, it may be a sign that you are being too stubborn.

Butterfly—The butterfly assists in positive change and transformation. It is useful for overcoming difficult circumstances and manifesting the prosperity you truly desire. To accelerate the change process, visualize yourself transforming into a butterfly as you chant "I am open to change!" The butterfly represents the more creative, playful side of life. Call upon the butterfly to make all your transitions more gentle and joyful.

Cat—Recognized as a magical and mystical animal from the beginning of time, the cat can be invoked when working prosperity magic or doing prosperity affirmations. The cat can be both loving and aloof. Consequently, it teaches us the balance between doing for ourselves and doing for others. Call upon the cat whenever your prosperity work requires setting emotional boundaries.

Cricket—The Chinese symbol of good luck and abundance, the cricket can be called to bless all that you do. The cricket is a small power animal, yet its appearance can mean giant leaps forward in your prosperity.

Cuckoo—The cuckoo is helpful in eliminating poverty patterns and creating a new, more prosperous life. The song of the cuckoo bird is unique and the cuckoo can help you uncover your unique talents that will lead you to a more prosperous life. The cuckoo is a benevolent power animal willing to assist you with your personal transformation.

Deer—A symbol of prosperity and sustenance to many of the world's ancient people, the deer helps you to be gentle with yourself during the unending process of prosperity work. It also assists in making positive change by teaching you to accept yourself exactly the way you are. Invoke the deer for all matters of emotional prosperity.

Donkey—Associated with the planet Saturn, the donkey can help instill discipline and perseverance and aid you in accessing your inner wisdom concerning prosperity. Call upon the donkey for opportunities and to get things done. However, be forewarned that the donkey will expect you to work for what you get.

Dragon—A power animal of supreme benevolent influence, the dragon has long been associated with prosperity and success. It is invoked for matters pertaining both to the physical and the spiritual realms. The dragon can help bring you your truest desires. Call upon the dragon to get past a creative block or when a matter is crucial.

Dragonfly—Invoke the dragonfly to positively transform anything in your life, including finances. The dragonfly helps to find the more colorful, playful side of yourself, and to move through your poverty patterns with ease and with joy.

Eagle—The eagle can help you soar in life. Invoke the eagle for good luck and victory in any endeavor. The eagle is pictured on American dollars. Therefore, you can call upon the eagle to manifest more dollars. The eagle can also help you translate your creative dreams into physical reality.

Frog—The frog gives the courage to accept new responsibilities and new ways in our lives. The frog can help you adjust to an ever-increasing prosperity. Call upon the frog to jump effortlessly to the next level of abundance. Because of its sheer numbers and green color, the frog is associated with all kinds of prosperity and abundance.

Goat—The goat carries you forward so that you can achieve your higher goals. The goat is associated with the sign of Capricorn and the ability to scale mountains and incredible obstacles. Call upon the goat to assist you in the long haul with all things of importance, and to help you through periods of heavy work or difficult dilemmas. The goat strengthens your resolve to be prosperous. It also can help you land on your feet when you are taking a risk or moving through a difficult situation.

Grasshopper—Considered an omen of good luck, the grasshopper can lead you to successful ventures or make your existing ventures successful. It can also help you make giant leaps forward in the pursuit of prosperity. Most grasshoppers are primarily green or brown, so it would be safe to say that you can call upon the grasshopper to manifest more money or material comforts.

Hawk—Famous for its keen eyesight, the hawk can help you to see both your poverty patterns and the new opportunities that lie before you. Hawks move swiftly, a sign that they can be called upon for rapid change, especially in times of crisis. The hawk can lead you toward the unfolding of your highest destiny and your greatest prosperity. However, be warned that the hawk has a serious and intense energy—invoke the hawk only if you mean business.

Hummingbird—The hummingbird inspires gratitude and positive thinking, and can help you taste the sweetness and joy of life. Although the hummingbird is tiny, its powerful wings beat with a mighty force, and it can help you to accomplish even the most impossible tasks with joy and ease.

Lion—The lion has long been a symbol of worldly power and success. Call upon the lion to develop your highest potential.

The lion can also help in times of adversity by giving you the confidence you need to claim your highest prosperity.

Phoenix—The phoenix rises from its ashes to fly once again. Call upon the phoenix to revitalize your finances or reawaken your dreams. The phoenix is a powerful ally for changing careers or making any other kind of major transition and is also helpful in working with poverty patterns.

Rabbit—The rabbit can help your prosperity move forward with leaps and bounds. Carrying a rabbit's foot was traditionally considered a way to bring good luck. By calling upon the spirit of the rabbit, you can multiply your own luck many times over!

Snake—The snake has the power to shed its skin and can help you transform your current situation into something more desirable. Invoke the snake to help you shed poverty patterns and grow new prosperity habits.

Spider—Long associated with creative power and manifestation because of its ability to weave webs, the spider is considered helpful when networking and making connections. Call upon the spider for success in all creative ventures, especially writing.

Turkey—The turkey is a symbol of harvest and the rewards of work well done. The turkey's tail feathers are green, brown, and copper. This indicates the turkey's spiritual connection with abundance and prosperity, especially of a material kind. Call upon the turkey to increase your blessings and to help you be more responsible with what you have been given.

www.crossingpress.com

BROWSE through the Crossing Press Web site for information on upcoming titles, new releases, and backlist books including brief summaries, excerpts, author information, reviews, and more.

SHOP our store for all of our books and, coming soon, unusual, interesting, and hard-to-find sideline items related to Crossing's best-selling books!

READ informative articles by Crossing Press authors on all of our major topics of interest.

SIGN UP for our e-mail newsletter to receive late-breaking developments and special promotions from The Crossing Press.

WATCH for a new look coming soon to the Crossing Press Web site!